ANSEL
ADAMS

THE SPIRIT OF WILD PLACES

ERIC PETER NASH

TODTRI

This book was designed and produced by
Todtri Productions Limited
P.O. Box 572 New York, NY 10116-0572
FAX: (212) 695-6984

Printed and bound in Singapore

ISBN 1-880908-37-9

Author: Eric Peter Nash

Publisher: Robert M. Tod
Book Designer: Mark Weinberg
Production Coordinator: Heather Weigel
Project Editor: Edward Douglas
Photo Editor: Ede Rothaus
Editors: Don Kennison, Linda Greer
Typesetting: Command-O, NYC

All photographs were supplied through the courtesy of The National Archives, Washington, D.C.
This book has been published without the assistance or endorsement of The Ansel Adams Publishing Rights Trust.

Selected Bibliography

Adams, Ansel, with Mary Street Alinder. *Ansel Adams: An Autobiography.* Boston: Little, Brown and Company, 1985.

Adams, Ansel. *Examples: The Making of 40 Photographs.* Boston: Little, Brown and Company, 1983.

Adams, Ansel, and Mary Street Alinder and Andrea Gray Stillman, eds. *Ansel Adams: Letters and Images 1916-1984.*
Boston: Little, Brown and Company, 1990.

Adams, Ansel. *Ansel Adams: The National Park Service Photographs.* New York: Abbeville Press, 1994.

Adams, Ansel, with Nancy Newhall. *This is the American Earth.* San Francisco: Sierra Club Books, 1992.

Conrat, Maisie and Richard Conrat. *Executive Order 9066: The Internment of 110,000 Japanese Americans.*
San Francisco: California Historical Society, 1972.

Heyman, Therese Tau, ed. *Seeing Straight: The f.64 Revolution in Photography.* Oakland, CA: The Oakland Museum, 1992.

Muir, John. *My First Summer in the Sierra.* San Frandisco: Sierra Club Books, 1990.

Newhall, Beaumont. *The History of Photography from 1839 to the Present Day.* New York: The Museum of Modern Art, 1964.

Newhall, Nancy, ed. *The Daybooks of Edward Weston.* New York: Aperture Foundation, 1981.

Newhall, Nancy. *The Eloquent Light* Ansel Adams, Volume I. San Francisco: Sierra Club, 1963.

Norman, Dorothy. *Alfred Stieglitz: An American Seer.* New York: Aperture Foundation, 1990.

Quinn, Karen E. and Theodore E. Stebbins Jr. *Ansel Adams: The Early Years.* Boston: The Museum of Fine Arts, 1991.

Read, Michael, ed. *Ansel Adams: New Light.* San Francisco: The Friends of Photography, 1993.

Schaefer, John P. *Ansel Adams Guide: Basic Techniques of Photography.* Boston: Little, Brown and Company, 1992.

Steichen, Edward. *The Family of Man.* New York: The Museum of Modern Art, 1983.

Wrigley, Richard. *Ansel Adams: Images of the American West.* New York: Smithmark, 1992.

FILMS

Berenice Abbott: A View of the 20th Century. Directed by Martha Wheelock and Kay Weaver. Ishtar Films, 1994.

Ansel Adams: Photographer. Directed by John Huszar. Pacific Arts Video, 1981.

CONTENTS

And this our life, exempt from public haunt,
Finds tongues in trees, books in the running brooks,
Sermons in stones, and good in everything.
Act II, scene i, As You Like It, William Shakespeare

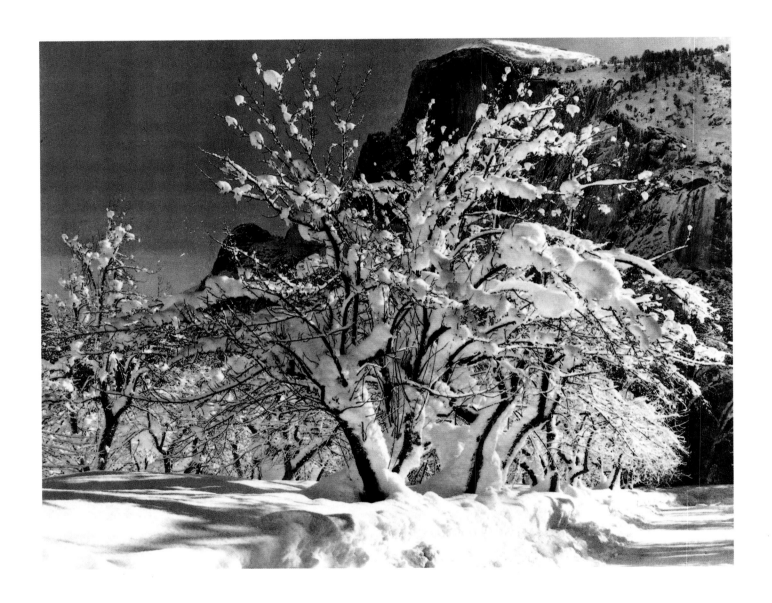

Half Dome, Apple Orchard, Yosemite National Park
This supernal image (c. 1930), one of Ansel Adams' most light-filled
and exuberant, was part of a series of images he presented in 1936
to persuade Congress to make Kings River Canyon, California, a national
park. A darkened sky sets off the dazzling highlights of sun on snow.

FIRST LIGHT

Sierra Dawn

Ansel Adams traced his first interest in photography to a bout of measles at the age of twelve. The boy was put to bed for two weeks in a darkened room to protect his eyes. The gap at the top of the drawn shades created a primitive camera obscura, where images of the outside world were projected across the ceiling—the principle by which a pinhole camera works. Curious about the phenomenon, Ansel asked his father Charles, who then opened up his Kodak Bullseye camera and showed him how the open shutter focused the light into a clear, upside-down image on a piece of semitransparent paper placed on the film plane.

Ansel, who was born on February 20, 1902 in San Francisco, had something of an unorthodox upbringing, completing his formal schooling in the eighth grade and thereafter training as a classical pianist. It would be many years before he would make a final choice between music and photography.

A seminal event in turning him toward photography was a family trip to California's Yosemite National Park in June of 1916, when Ansel was fourteen. The teenager had pored over the purple prose and glorious tales of cowboys and Indians in a book called *In the Heart of the Sierras*, by Dr. Lafayette Bunnell. The day of the family's arrival was filled with dazzling impressions that would last a lifetime: the pervasive sunlight, the cool ferns and grasses, the green depths of the rivers, and what Ansel remembered in his autobiography as "the unbelievable glow of a Sierra dawn. A new era began for me."

While they were at Yosemite, Ansel's parents gave him his first camera, a Kodak Box Brownie No. 1. The combination of subject and camera would prove irresistible. Ansel took his first picture of the Half Dome cliff while hurtling head first upside down during a fall from a crumbling tree stump! He did manage to get a reasonably sharp negative from the experience. The man who developed the roll was curious as to how that one shot proved to be upside down on the roll. Ansel explained, but felt afterwards that the developer always thought he was a little nuts.

Ansel spent the summers of the next few years blithely taking snapshots of all the manifold sights of Yosemite National Park. His intent was primarily documentary rather than artistic or expressive, but as he noted, "The snapshot is not as simple a statement as some may believe. It represents something that each of us has seen—more as human beings than photographers—and wants to keep as a memento, a special thing encountered."

At the same time, Ansel was being introduced to the darkroom, a step that separates the ham amateur from the professional photographer, especially in black-and-white photography. He got a part-time job with Frank Dittman, a San Francisco neighbor, working at his photo-finishing business for $2 a day.

At this stage Ansel saw himself as little more than an enthusiastic hobbyist but he was beginning the slow, step-by-step procedure of developing an intuitive sense for the mechanics of exposure and printing. Even then Ansel had an inkling of what the expressive powers of a photograph could be. He could see an image clearly in his mind's eye, but did not know yet how to capture it on paper. A view of Baker Beach gave a foretaste of the emotional impact a picture could convey, with its massive, dark cliffs towering over the ocean horizon and the light segmenting the cliff faces into clean planes. The scene remained with him as an emblem of something he wanted to achieve as a photographer.

Adams came nearer to getting what he wanted with the picture Diamond Cascade, Yosemite National Park (1920), which was of a small cascade of water in Yosemite's Tenayas Canyon. His conception was not simply to capture a material representation of the falls but somehow to express the inherent power of water in motion, the glimmer of light on the surface, and the lightness of the spray. The fast-moving water appears as a light gray mass set against a somber background, with highlights of foaming white water. The abstract, dynamic composition of blacks, whites, and tones of gray adds another layer of meaning to the picture because the eye cannot take them in all at once and is forced to travel again and again over the surface, mimicking the flow of the water.

Key to the success of the photo was first visualizing the dark value of the background that sets off the play of sunlight in water. Adams has written that he achieved this unity of subject and form in only a few photographs from that era.

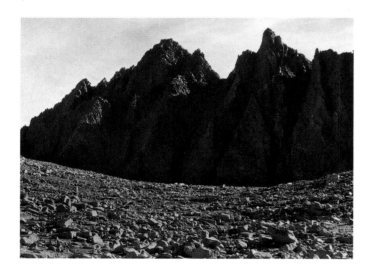

Bishop Pass

This image can be seen as a forerunner of Adams' later, masterful photograph, Mount Williamson, Sierra Nevada, from Manzanar, California (1944). In both pictures there is a dramatic change in scale from foreground to background. Here, the center of attention is the curved horizon line between the light gray foreground and the shadowed peaks.

The Transcendent World

Ansel spent his next four summers working as a custodian for the Sierra Club's headquarters, the LeConte Memorial Lodge. In 1920 he urgently telegraphed his father: "Can buy burro for twenty including outfit. Can sell at end of season for ten. Fine investment and useful. Wire immediately as offer is for today only."

His letters from the period are filled with an exalted love of the wilderness that would carry over into his photography: "I look on the lines and forms of the mountains and all other aspects of nature as if they were but the vast expression of ideas within the Cosmic Mind. . . . The world has suddenly opened up to me with tremendous and dazzling effect." The effect of the spirit of place on an artist has been well documented. He described a mystical moment on Mount Clark, when the clear, early-morning light made every detail of the scene luminous and sharp, and the world seemed to fall away, giving him a keen awareness of the pure quality of light itself.

Ansel's correspondence in many ways mirrors the emotions expressed by an earlier American naturalist, John Muir, who called the High Sierra "the Range of Light." Muir, too, experienced a dreamlike suspension of time in the high mountains. In his classic book *First Summer in the Sierra* (1911) Muir wrote: "Another glorious Sierra day in which one seems to be dissolved and absorbed and set pulsing onward we know not where. Life seems neither long nor short, and we take no more heed to save time or make haste than do the trees and stars. This is true freedom, a good practical sort of immortality."

Ansel explored Yosemite in the days before European alpine climbing techniques had reached the United States. The gentle humor of the man can be seen in the 1981 documentary film *Ansel Adams: Photographer*, as he recalls the period and his climbing: "In the early days we nearly killed ourselves because we didn't have any knowledge at all of climbing techniques, and we'd tie ourselves together with a piece of window sash cord and climb together. If one fell it would undoubtedly pull the other one off, but some way or another we just

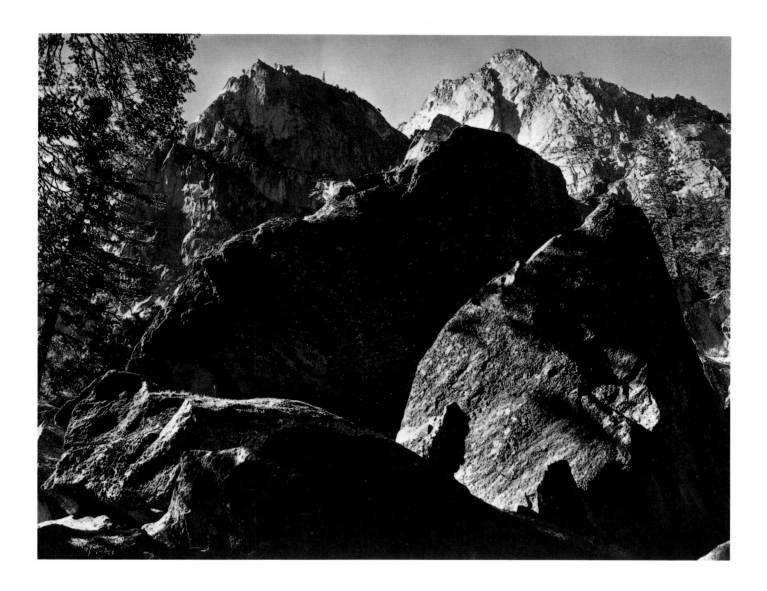

thought that if we were tied together, we were safe."

Adams recalls one photograph he made on a sunny spring afternoon in 1927 that forever changed his understanding of the medium of photography. He lugged his forty-pound camera pack—which included a Korona view camera, an array of lenses, two filters, six holders with twelve glass plates, and a wooden tripod—up to an area of Yosemite known as the Diving Board, which commanded a view of the park's most spectacular sight, the face of the Half Dome cliff. Down to his last two slides, Ansel set up his camera at mid-afternoon with a sharp 8 1/2-inch Zeiss Tessar lens, which he covered with a standard K2 yellow filter to darken the bright sky.

Grand Sentinel

Typically, Adams used a lens with a long focal length to flatten the planes of his subject into a more abstract composition. Grand Sentinel is a bold composition of black and gray planes meeting at sharply defined edges. The forms draw the eye upward to the distant peaks.

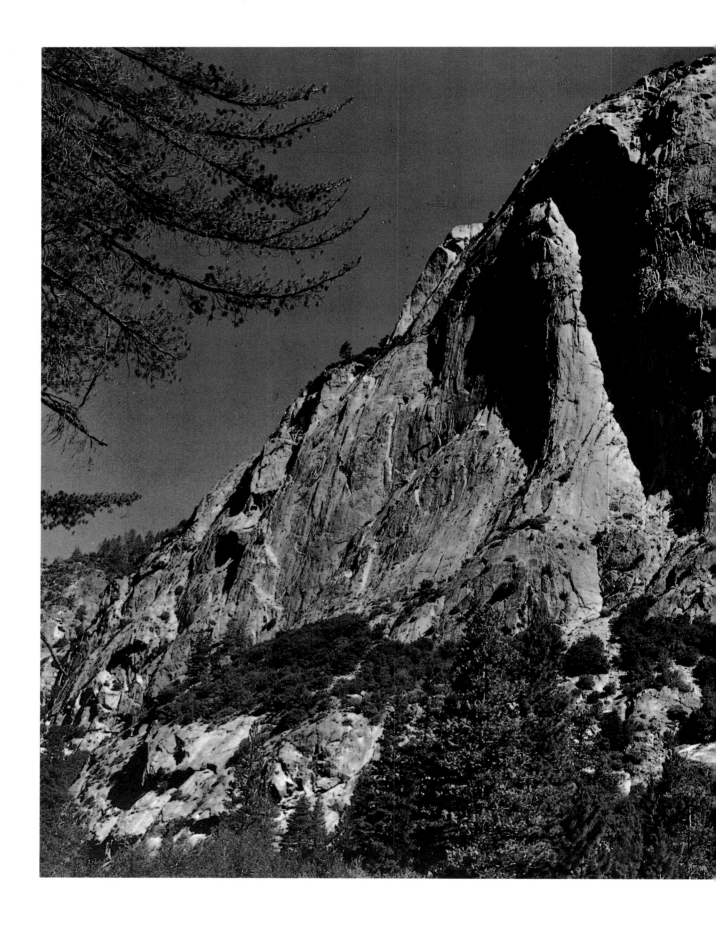

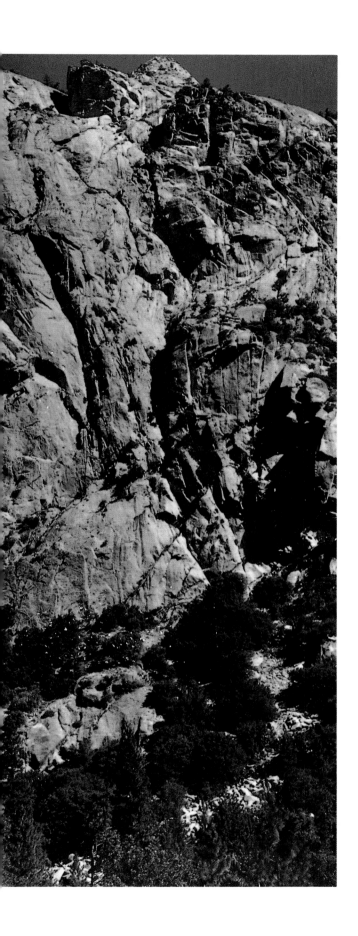

As he was replacing the slide to take his final shot of the day he thought about the feeling he wanted the final print to convey, the starkness of the monumental shape before him. Ansel summoned up a mental image of how the cliff would look in the final print, with the moody cliff set against a darkened sky and the etched sharpness of the snow-capped Tenaya Peak in the far distance. Only a deep red filter would make the reality before him appear as he envisioned it. He replaced the conventional choice of a K2 yellow filter with a red Wratten No. 29(F), which required increasing the exposure by a factor of 16 times, and released the shutter.

Not until he developed the plate that evening did he realize the significance of his accomplishment. He wrote later: "I had achieved my first true visualization! I had been able to realize a desired image not the way the subject appeared in reality but how it felt to me and how it must appear in the finished print."

What was a naturalistic rendition of the scene became an image of stark power and beauty. In the photograph the cliff becomes something elemental, looming out of the darkened sky. The viewer becomes aware of the chilly void of space, the solidity and massiveness of the rock face, and the etched perfection of the snowy peak in the background. The sharper contrast brings out hidden detail, like the fine shadows cast by the tree in the foreground, an eye-blink in time compared with the eternal presence of the black cliff face. The eye is drawn from the deep black shadows of the cliff across the gray tonalities of rock to the dazzling whiteness of the snow, emphasizing the thrust and sweep of the cliff. The scene is so tangible you can almost hear the

North Dome, Kings River Canyon

The barren, somewhat lunar quality of this image
recalls Ansel's earlier *Monolith, The Face of Half Dome,
Yosemite National Park* (1927), which he felt was his
first successful visualization. In both pictures, stark black
shadows give a feeling of massiveness to the cliff faces.

soughing of the tree branches, the wind across the expanses of rock, and the settling of the snow cover in the sunlight. The stillness of eternity is captured in the fraction of a second it took to snap the camera's shutter.

During his summers at Yosemite, Adams made the acquaintance of Harry Best, owner of Best's Photography Studio, one of the handful of private businesses in the park. One plus at Best's was a piano for Ansel to practice on. Another attraction was Harry's beautiful young daughter, Virginia, who shared Ansel's enthusiasm for the outdoors and accompanied him on his photographic treks through the park.

Ansel courted her for six years and they were married on a snowy January 2, 1928, at her father's studio. The bride wore black because she didn't have time to buy a wedding dress, and Ansel wore knickers with basketball shoes. Wedding photos discreetly show him only from the knees up. A son, Michael, was born in 1932, and their daughter, Anne, arrived two years later.

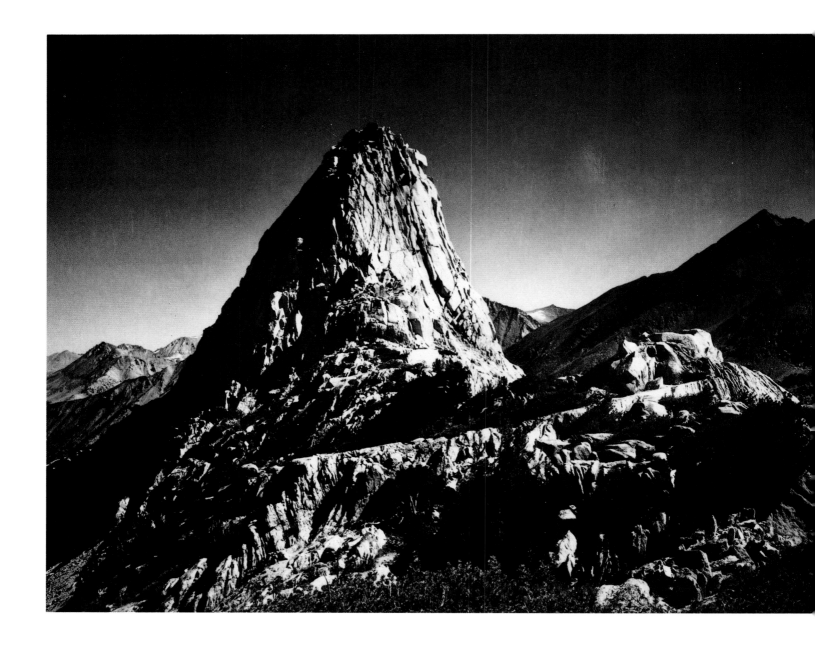

The Modern World

Adams' meeting with the photographer Paul Strand in New Mexico in the summer of 1930 was a critical juncture in the development of his thinking and work. Strand offered to show Ansel some of his negatives, using a sheet of white paper and the bright New Mexico sunlight for a light box. Ansel recalls the moment as transformative: "They were glorious negatives: full, luminous shadows and strong high values in which subtle passages of tone were preserved. The compositions were extraordinary: perfect, uncluttered edges and beautifully distributed shapes that he had carefully selected and interpreted as forms—simple, yet of great power."

Adams returned to San Francisco with a determination to make photography, rather than music, his career. Paul Strand had provided the vital link—between a modernist technique and the natural subject matter—that allowed Ansel's thinking to fall into place. Modernism in photography is often associated with modernist content, such as Charles Sheeler's gleaming steel machinery, skyscrapers, locomotives—motion and progress of all kinds. But in the 1920s Strand turned away from the culture of the machine and applied his clean-edged, sharply-defined technique to photos of New England and New Mexico.

This combination is what Adams perceived in the negatives Strand had showed him. Ansel's own budding modernist sensibilities can be seen in his admiration for such qualities as "perfect, uncluttered edges" and the great power of simple forms. It was a further step in his rejection of the misty romanticism of pictorialist photographers such as Edward

Fin Dome

Dark and light planes are dramatically juxtaposed on the two faces of the dome, set against a deep gray sky. The vast sky emphasizes the vertical angularity and isolation of the rock. The dramatic tone of Adams' photos was influential in impelling Congress to declare Kings River Canyon a National Park in 1940.

Steichen and other "fuzzie-wuzzies," as Adams referred to them.

In 1933 Ansel wrote what amounts to a fan letter to Strand, saying that he was psychologically and physically moved by his images, and that "I believe you have made the one perfect and complete definition of photography." Adams would be struck by the clarity of Strand's prints at a later meeting in New York. Strand used toners to make the whites glisten against marvelously deep blacks, a practice Ansel would adopt to bring out the luminous passages in his prints.

There were special properties of light in the regions in which both men worked. The New Mexico desert and the High Sierras are lands of great extremes and stark contrasts. John Muir, with a true photographer's eye for the emotional quality of light, described a magical scene on the forest floor in *First Summer in Yosemite*: ". . . low soft and lovely the light streaming through this living ceiling, revealing the arching branching ribs and veins of the fronds as the framework of countless panes of pale green and yellow plant-glass nicely fitted together—a fairyland created out of common fernstuff."

Group f/64

Adams brought his evangelical zeal for a new, modernist-influenced school of photography to a meeting in 1932 of like-minded souls at the Berkeley, California, home of the photographer Willard Van Dyke. Also in attendance were Edward Weston, Imogen Cunningham, Henry Swift, Sonia Noskowiak, and John Paul Edwards. Ansel spoke animatedly about the need to move away from pictorialism toward a new form of "pure" or "straight" photography. On another night, they looked for a name for their nascent group and came up with Group f/64, named after the smallest aperture stop on a camera lens. The name is significant.

Members of the group were fond of shooting at f/64, which gives the greatest depth of field and overall clarity of focus to a picture. Ansel would use this amazing "God's eye" overall focus to grandly operatic effect in later works, such as the well-known

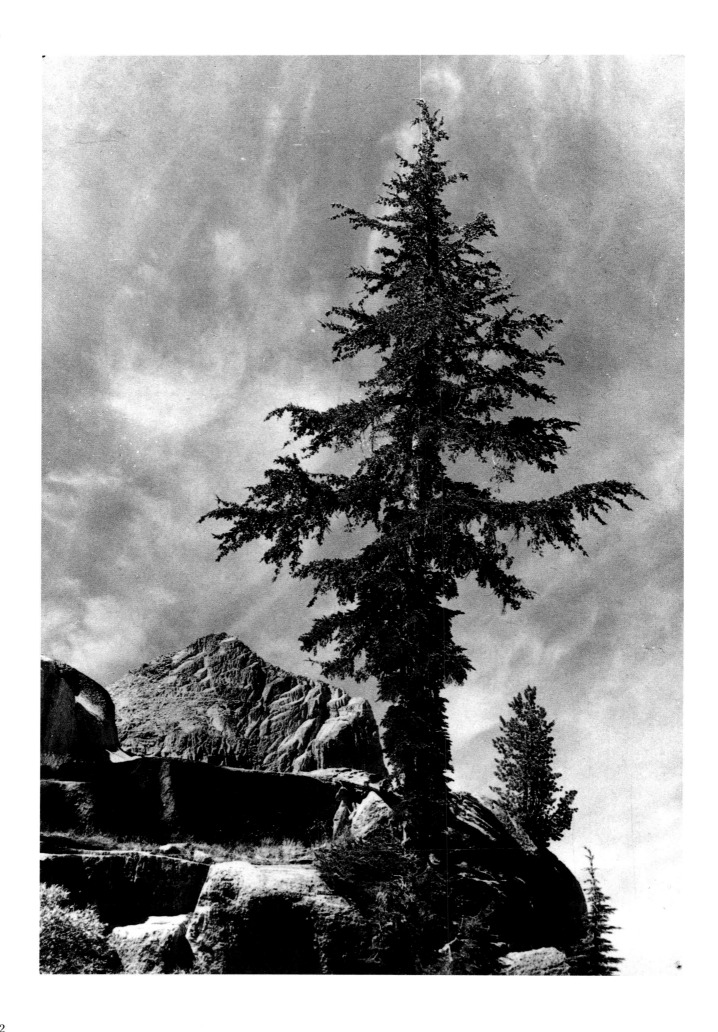

Moonrise, Hernandez, New Mexico (1941), in which everything from here to eternity seems to be in crisp focus. And *Winter Sunrise, Sierra Nevada, From Lone Pine, California* (1944) surely must be how God sees the world, with everything in perfect focus from the tender detail of the black horse grazing in a patch of light in the foreground to the farthest snow-covered peaks. Adams once remarked, "Sometimes I think I do get to places just when God's ready to have somebody click the shutter!"

For Ansel the essence of the group's aesthetic philosophy was what he called straight photography, meaning that photographs should be true to their own medium rather than imitations of other art forms. The group rebelled against the soft-focus, pictorial style of photography in vogue in the 1920s, in which the primary purpose was to establish the "artistic" legitimacy of the medium by slavishly imitating great paintings. Ansel and the f/64 group were interested in an aesthetic based on the intrinsic qualities of the photographic process itself. At this point, he gave up printing his negatives on the textured paper he had been using in favor of the smooth, glossy printing paper used by Paul Strand and Edward Weston in order to extract every possible detail from the negative.

After being turned down by the major fine-art galleries in San Francisco, the group had a triumphant and tradition-breaking opening at the M. H. deYoung Museum in San Francisco on November 15, 1932. The group's manifesto for the show is worth reproducing in full to illustrate the modernist bent of their thinking.

An Unnamed Peak

A sweeping evergreen fills the vertical and horizontal axes against a detailed sky of wispy clouds. The overall effect is of joyful upward motion, space, and freedom, accentuated by the breathtakingly empty space at the lower right of the frame. The tree appears as a glorious kite sailing over the high mountains.

GROUP F/64 MANIFESTO

The name of this Group is derived from a diaphragm number of the photographic lens. It signifies to a large extent the qualities of clearness and definition of the photographic image which is an important element in the work of members of this Group.

The chief object of the Group is to present in frequent shows what it considers the best contemporary photography of the West; in addition to the showing of the work of its members, it will include prints from other photographers who evidence tendencies in their work similar to that of the Group.

Group f/64 is not pretending to cover the entire field of photography or to indicate through its selection of members any deprecating opinion of the photographers who are not included in its shows. There are a great number of serious workers in photography whose style and technique does not relate to the metier of the Group.

Group f/64 limits its members and invitational names to those workers who are striving to define photography as an art form by simple and direct presentation through purely photographic methods. The Group will show no work at any time that does not conform to its standards of pure photography. Pure photography is defined as possessing no qualities of technique, composition or idea, derivative of any other art form. The production of the "Pictorialist," on the other hand, indicates a devotion to principles of art which are directly related to painting and the graphic arts.

The members of Group f/64 believe that photography, as an art form, must develop along lines defined by the actualities and limitations of the photographic medium, and must always remain independent of ideological conventions of art and aesthetics that are reminiscent of a period and culture antedating the growth of the medium itself.

The Group will appreciate information regarding any serious work in photography that has escaped its attention, and is favorable towards establishing itself as a Forum of Modern Photography.

Like other modernist movements of the era, such as the Internationalist style in architecture, Group f/64 sought to sever all ties with what they saw as the dead weight of the past and to create a brand new art form. The parallels with the architectural movement of Internationalism are telling. The architects Le Corbusier and Mies van der Rohe sought to eliminate all false historical revivalism in building design, and to strip the buildings down to an aesthetic of pure functionalism by making the building's form reveal how it was built.

Adams was doing virtually the same thing in photography. Historicism was rejected by ridding photographs of any reference to the earlier medium of painting: no more gauzy, soft-focus portraits in imitation of the Impressionists; no more lighting and composition lifted from Rembrandt; no pictures chosen solely for the sentimentality of the subject matter. In the same way that the Internationalists wanted to evince the inner workings of buildings, Ansel attempted to build an aesthetic on the photographic process itself rather than to hide it with pictorial window dressing. His compositions were based on light, form, and tonal value rather than on any second-hand concepts of beauty.

A Portrait of Ansel

Ansel Adams has been dismissed in some contemporary critical circles as a kind of poster boy for the Sierra Club. Indeed, the paucity of critical literature on the artist, with the exception of a few books such as *Ansel Adams: New Light, Essays on His Legacy and Legend by the Friends of Photography*, illuminates the serious misunderstanding of his work by present-day critics. He is often seen merely as a landscape photographer of little interest in regard to today's postmodern concerns.

Sometimes, however, the public will understand something that the critics miss. Something keeps drawing people back to Adams' images, and it is not simply that they are pretty pictures of nature. Countless nature photographers have been consigned to the scrapbook of history. Part of Ansel's appeal is the complexity of his images. There is a

tension and a sense of mystery in much of his work, as there is in all great works of art.

This tension derives in part from his use of natural scenes to produce a purely modernist composition. For example, the dunes in *Sand Dunes, Sunrise, Death Valley National Monument, California* (1948) are perfectly comprehensible as sand dunes, but they are also a marvelous, clean-edged, pure-formed abstract composition of blacks and whites and tones of gray. As soon as the viewer sees it as sand dunes, the mind is drawn to the purely abstract shapes, and then back once more to nature. The picture is in constant flow, just as sand dunes themselves are. This transcendental unity of form and subject is what brings us back for another look.

Ansel also has been misunderstood as being a rather chilly, unemotional photographer, interested only in his Zone Theory of the gradation of tones in black-and-white photography. This was a problem from the first, when Ansel announced his intentions of Purist photography. In response to a broadside called "The Fallacies of Pure Photography" by his arch-nemesis William Mortensen, Ansel countered that objective photography in no way meant that it was unemotional. Ansel believed that an objective viewpoint was the only way to convey strong emotions.

It may be that the emotional content of Ansel's photographs jars the postmodern sensibility: they are not the angst-ridden images of Diane Arbus, and they do not use the dissociative techniques of someone like Nick Waplington nor the pseudo-historical appliqué of Cindy Sherman. Rather, they go back to the earlier epoch of the New England

Mount Winchell

Vertical bands of deep shadow accentuate the upward thrust of the rock face, complementing the overall vertical composition of the image. The viewer is led to follow the lines of shadow up from the finely detailed slag at the base and then to scan the image horizontally, comparing the visually exciting contrasts of shadows and highlights. The total effect is dynamic, calling the viewer back to seek new detail.

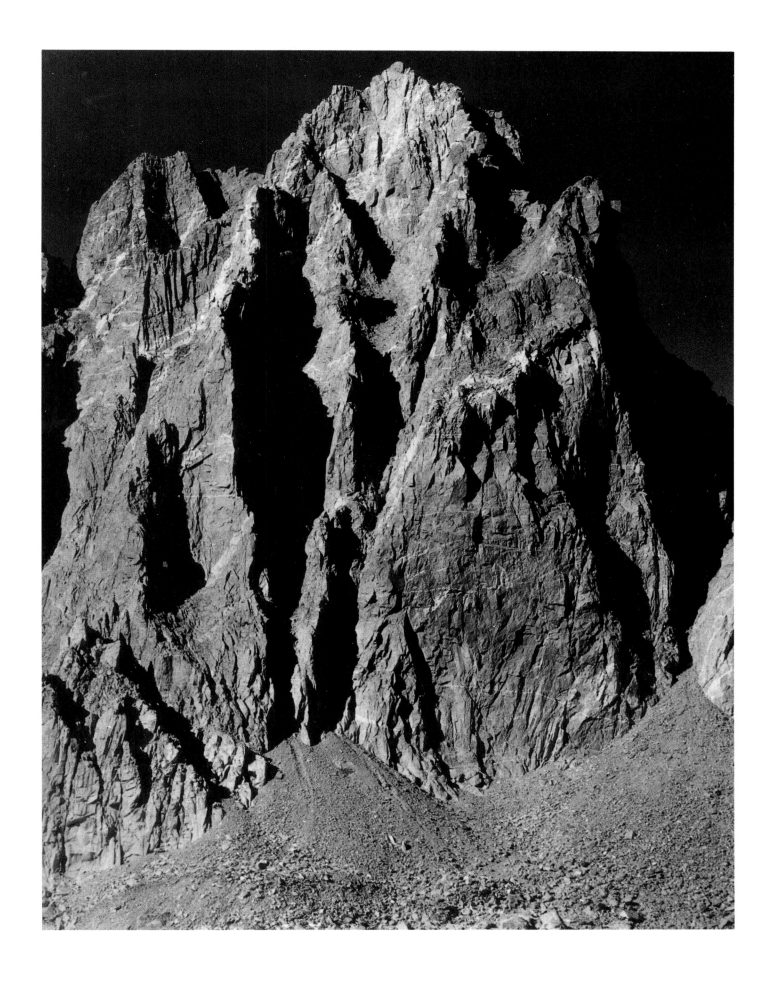

Transcendentalist thinkers who viewed nature with reverence and awe as an unfolding, limitless joy buoyed by a sense of unity among the smallest and the greatest.

Conveying his feelings at the time of taking the picture was the whole point for Ansel. In answer to critics who said that there were never any people in his pictures, Ansel would reply that there were always two people in his pictures: the photographer and the viewer. *Self Portrait, Monument Valley, Utah* (1958) is a perfect expression of his relationship to the photo. He and his view camera appear as a somewhat indistinct shadow against a sharply etched rock face. The thrown shadow puts the viewer right in the picture—it could almost be one's own shadow. You can just about hear the photographer's excited voice in your ear, "Look! Look here!" The white fissures in the rock face crackle like lightning bolts all around. The scale of the background is indeterminate. Are we looking at a near surface, or at a towering shadow over a vast plain below? In the picture, the photographer is the shadow—he is part of the play of light and dark. When Ansel Adams shows us his photos, he is showing us himself.

Two earlier self-portraits show a similar affinity between the man and the medium. In *Self Portrait in a Victorian Mirror, Atherton, California* (1936) Ansel appears as a bug-eyed creature behind his view camera in the reflection of a Victorian bull's-eye mirror. Everything is in crisp focus, from the flocked wallpaper behind the mirror to the deep background of the reflected room. Ansel seems to be looking out at us through the lens of the mirror, just as he looks at us through the camera. Viewer and subject switch places, and it is we who are looking out at the world through a lens. Ansel's work is full of such Alice in Wonderland-style shifts in viewpoint. As viewers we are involved in his photos.

Self Portrait, San Francisco (1936) portrays the photographer gazing into the lens of his camera upon a shelf, with a mounted print of *Dead Tree near Little Five Lakes, Sequoia National Park, California* (c. 1932) between them. It is almost as if he took a picture of himself and it came out as the tree. Or was the tree what the photographer saw through the camera? Print, camera, and man are arranged in a dynamic trinity, each entity overlapping, so that it is difficult to say where one starts and another leaves off.

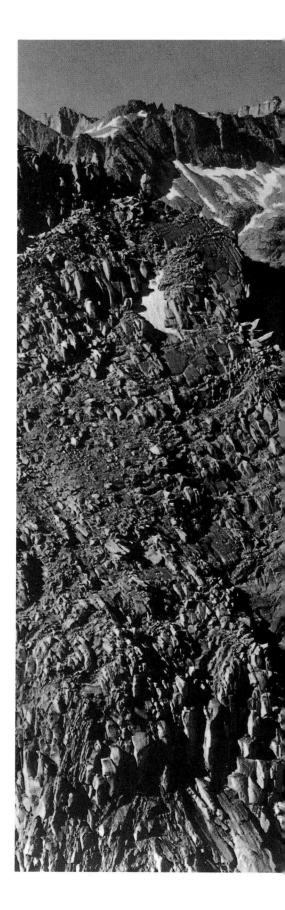

Mount Brewer

This is a strongly two-dimensional image because of the flattening effect of a long lens and the cropped sky. The eye probes the massed rock surfaces for a sense of depth, finding it only in the changed scale of the far peaks on the right. A black chasm dominates the lower part of the frame, with elongated tendrils of shadow that lead the viewer back over the broken rock surface.

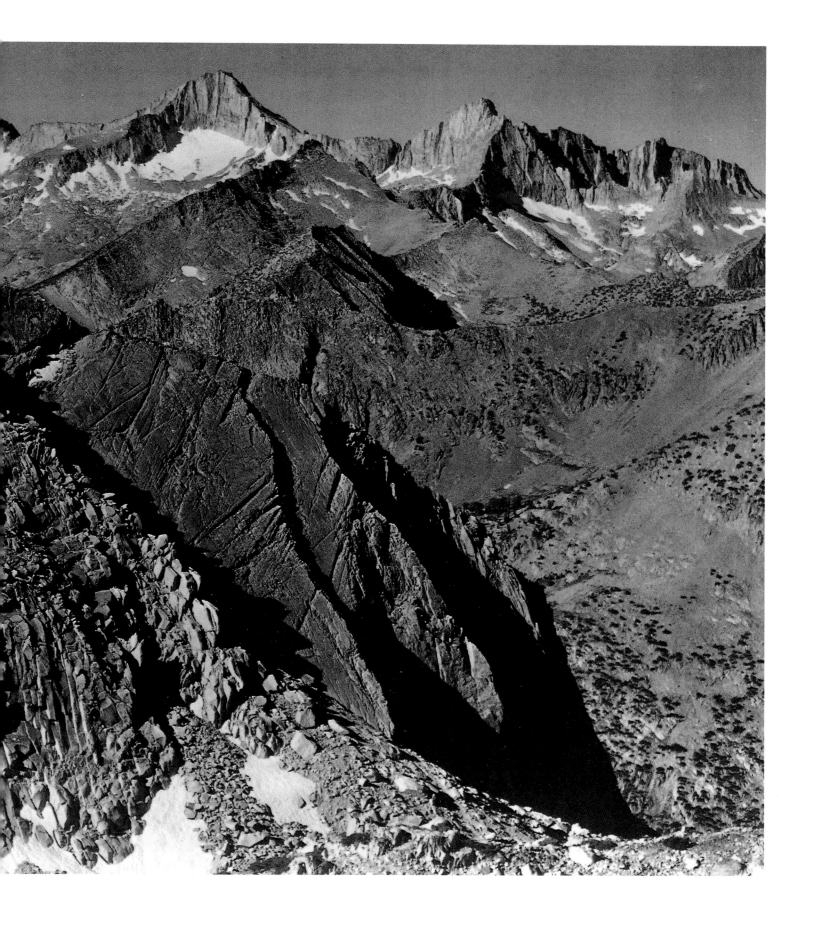

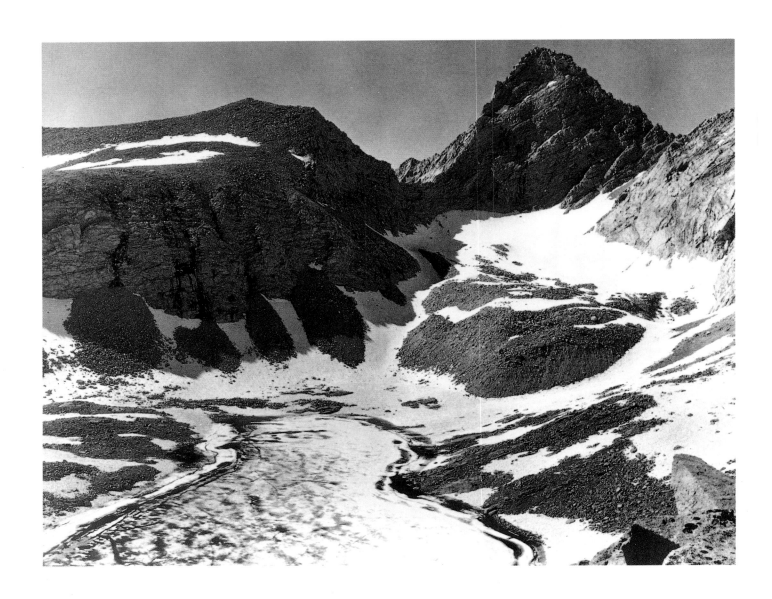

Junction Peak

This is a dazzling image, not only for the highlights of snow on the upper left
that seem so bright you almost want to put on a visor to look at them, but also
because of the wonderfully complex midground where dark rock, shadowed
snow, and sunlit snow form abstract, alternating zones. Ansel's modernist
sensibilities are fully at work here, as he boldly explores this clean-edged pattern.

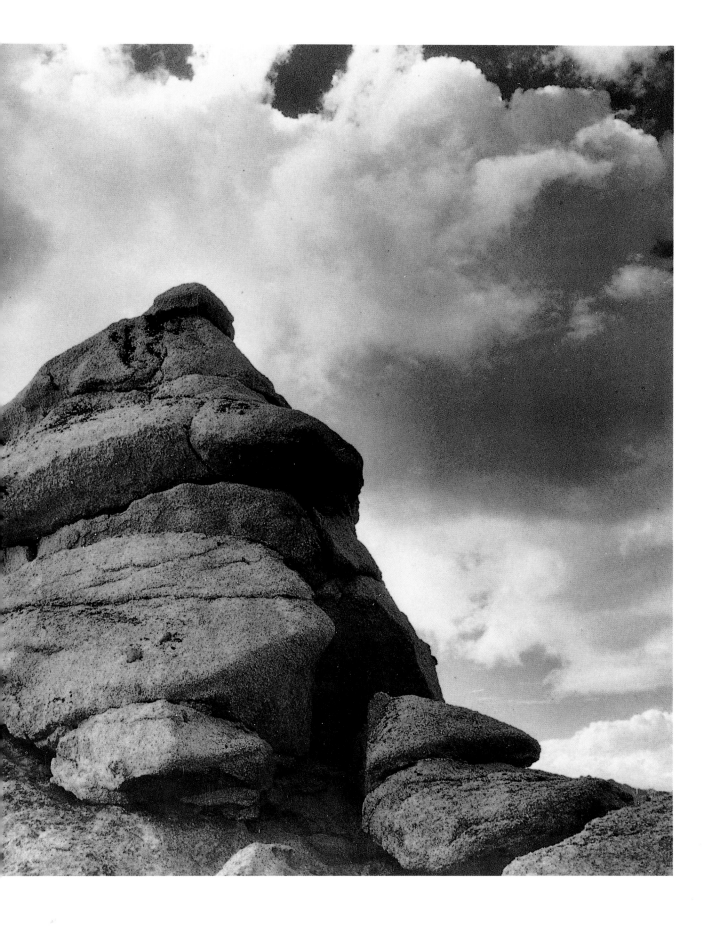

cameras. Photographers at the time preferred to make contact prints directly from an 8-by-10 negative, which yielded the absolutely sharpest print. With subsequent refinements in the enlarging process, and the resultant clarity of enlarged prints, 35mm work became the norm.

One immediate byproduct of the switch from bulky view cameras that required cumbersome tripods to the lighter, more portable 35mm cameras was a liberation of the whole subject matter of photography. In the same way that faster, more light-sensitive film stocks allowed photographers to go beyond still lifes and posed portraits to look at the world unfolding around them, the unobtrusive 35mm camera let photographers penetrate more deeply into the social sphere, giving rise to the school of "street photography" led by Garry Winogrand and Robert Frank, and to the omnipresence of photojournalism.

In fact, Stieglitz may have been smiling at the novelty of seeing the younger photographer with one of these new cameras. "If I had a camera like that," he stated, "I would close this place up and be out on the streets of the city!" Then, on a sadder note: "I guess it is too late for me. I leave the job to you young people."

From the last decade of the nineteenth century, Stieglitz was perhaps the prime mover in gaining recognition for photography as a legitimate art form, independent from the graphic arts and painting. His Photo-Secession group, founded in 1902 and dedicated to the advancement of photography as a means of artistic expression, was widely influential and critically successful in America and Europe. When asked by the chairman of the National Arts Club what exactly Photo-Secession represented, Stieglitz, never modest, replied, "Yours truly for the present, and there'll be others when the show opens." But he did go on to reveal the profundity of his thinking: "In Europe—in Germany and Austria—splits have occurred in art circles, the moderns calling themselves Secessionists. So Photo-Secession hitches up with the art world."

Stieglitz was a champion of the nascent modern art movement in Europe and brought an exhibit by Henri Matisse before a surprisingly hostile New York audience. A critic for the New York Evening Mail went so far as to say, "On the strength of these things of subterhuman hideousness, I shall try to put Henri Matisse out of my mind for the present." Stieglitz also found much in common with the avant-garde artist Francis Picabia, and gave him his first American one-man exhibition in March of 1913.

Ansel and the Art World

Stieglitz was sufficiently prescient to realize what the consequences of the new art form of photography would be for the traditional form of painting. Many painters of the time feared that the photographic image would render painting obsolete, but Stieglitz saw that painting could instead be liberated from the merely representational and move on to something new: modern or abstract art. Stieglitz was thus radically modern in all his thinking, both in seeing photography as a new medium with no debt to the past and in foreseeing the consequences for modern painting.

Stieglitz—like Adams—came from a nineteenth-century aesthetic, which viewed art in Romantic terms, as a quest for truth and beauty. For Stieglitz photography was "an entire philosophy and way of life—a religion. . . . If we are not truthful, we cannot help one another. Where there is no conscience, there can be no art. The goal of the artist is to be truthful and then share his truthfulness with others."

Indeed, it is the directness of Stieglitz's gaze that makes his images so enduringly powerful. Take note, for example, of the natural, unforced composition and dynamic power of *The Car Horses* (1893); the breathtaking spareness and elegance of *Spring Showers, New York* (1902); or the direct transmission of emotion to the viewer in the marvelously dense *Winter, Fifth Avenue, New York* (1893). Stieglitz, the most undemonstrative of men, was—again, like Adams—caught up in the fever to express himself on film. His motto was always, "Where there is light, one can photograph." When he showed the wet negative of *Winter* to his colleagues at the New York Society

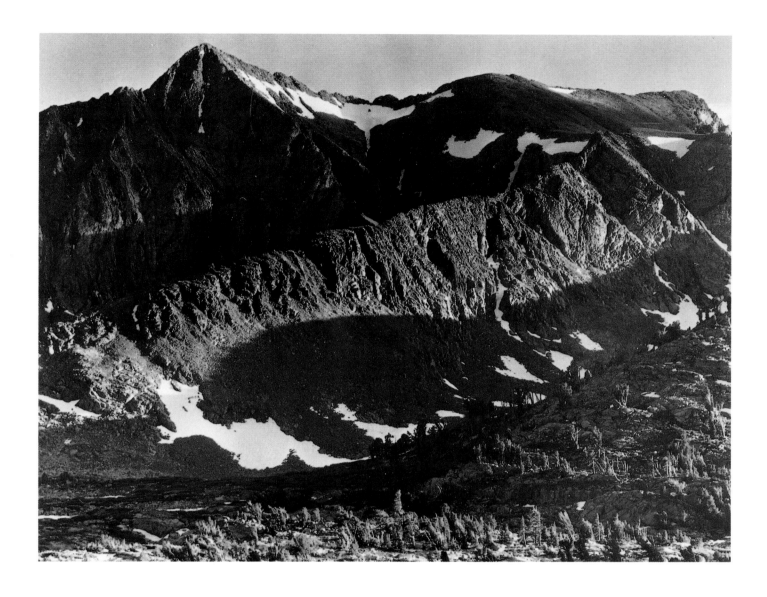

of Amateur Photographers, he was ridiculed for producing a blurry and unsharp image. Stieglitz declared that his negative was the beginning of a new era, which in fact it was.

Stieglitz was one of the first photographers to be recognized by an American art museum. The Boston Museum of Fine Arts owned a collection of his photos, but during the 1920s Stieglitz held out for years, due to nonpayment, over donating a collection to New York's Metropolitan Museum of Art. Finally, Stieglitz gave the Met a set of his limited prints for their first photography collection. He was unhappy about the lack of payment but believed that the break with the past on the part of the Met

Peak above Woody Lake
In this horizontally composed image with strong diagonal elements, the highlights are on the central rocky ridge. The encroaching shadow on the lighter rock face has an almost tangible weight of its own. The diagonal motif is repeated by the ridge in the foreground, the line of shadow, the edge of the bright cliff against the darker mountain, and finally by the profile of the mountain against the sky.

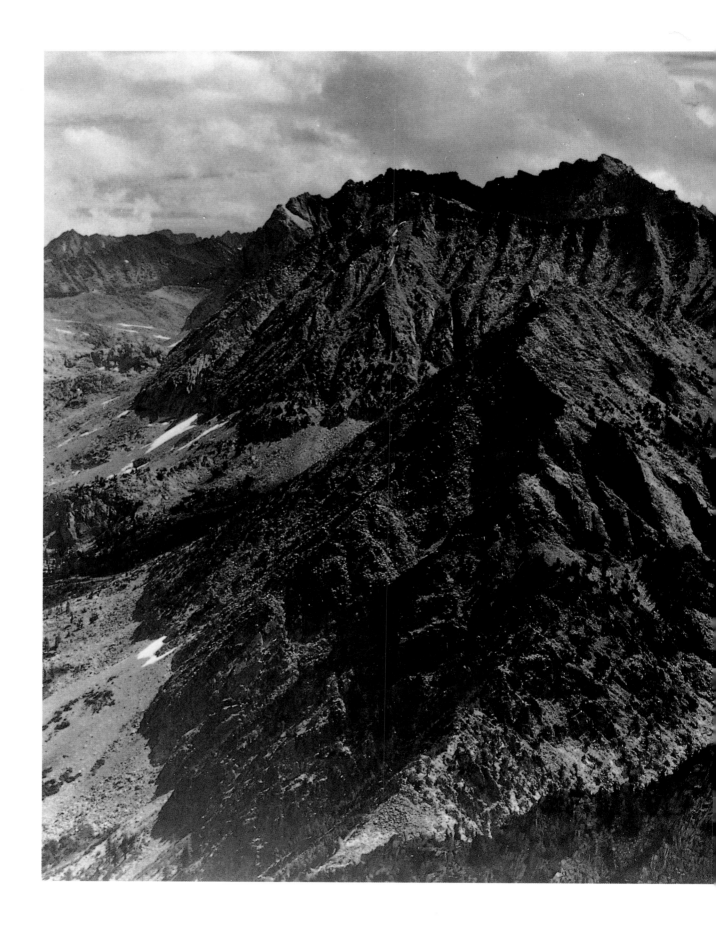

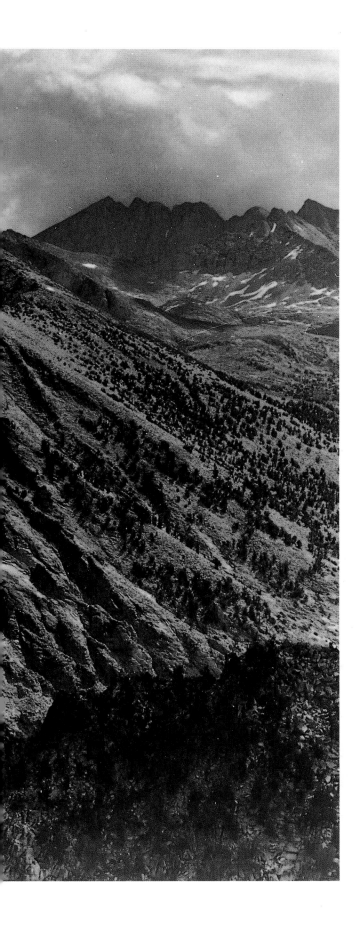

would do much to further the cause of photography. Stieglitz, however, would end up having little to do with one of the major exponents of modern photography in the country, perhaps because he felt it diminished the status of his own gallery, An American Place.

During the 1930s, An American Place was a magnet for artists in all fields. Visitors included the writer Sherwood Anderson, the poets William Carlos Williams, Hart Crane, e. e. cummings, and Marianne Moore, the painter Marcel Duchamp, the composers Edgard Varèse and Aaron Copland, and Clifford Odets and Stella Adler, members of the Group Theater.

Adams was proud to be in the Stieglitz fold. After his opening at An American Place, Ansel wrote enthusiastically to Virginia about the success of his show. He noted that seven pictures were already sold at an average of $30, and that one of them, *The White Tombstone, Laurel Hill Cemetery, San Francisco* (1936), a powerful image of a weathered headstone set against an eerie, almost solarized-looking background, sold for $100. It would be many years before photographers received prices in the thousands of dollars for their prints. Such a thing was unimaginable at the time.

In his autobiography, Ansel recalled a representative of the Internal Revenue Service at odds over the evaluation of a Stieglitz print, *The City at Night*, which sold for $15,500 in 1946. The IRS man at first insisted it had to be a painting or at least a photograph of a great painting, as he obviously believed that a photograph in itself surely could not be worth so much.

From Windy Point

The highlights in this exalted view of a windswept, rocky promontory are not in the sky but in the bright patches of snow in the far background. The effect is to bring out the depth and texture of the image. Deep black shadows on the far rocks provide a strong contrast.

A New Art in a New Land

Interestingly, the photos Ansel chose for his New York exhibitions were atypical of the epic scale of his later works, such as *Mount Williamson, Sierra Nevada, from Manzanar, California* (1944). He showed instead close-ups, with a few exceptions, such as *Monolith.* There were even photographs of people, like the portrait of the San Francisco journalist Carolyn Anspacher.

This portrait of a woman's head in three-quarter profile shows Ansel's mastery of classical forms of composition. The modeling of light on the head gives it the mass and solidity of a Greek sculpture, whereas the balance of highlights on the skin, the tonality of the shadows, and the clear, deep blacks of her pupils announce that this is a thoroughly modern portrait of a young woman. The eye bounces back and forth from the classical associations of portraiture to the picture of a living person.

Ansel later wrote of his style of portraiture: "I photograph heads as I would photograph sculpture . . . the head or figure is clearly presented as an object, the edge, mass, texture of the skin, and the general architecture of the face and form is revealed with great intensity . . . the expression—many possible expressions—are implied." As with his landscapes, he found complete depth of field to be essential, and felt that portraits in which one element of the face was in sharp focus and the rest blurry were extremely disturbing.

In his revealing book *Examples: The Making of 40 Photographs*, Adams wrote that he was satisfied with the portrait, though it had gained the sobriquet "The Great Stone Face." In fact, some believed it to be a picture of a statue's head. "This actually pleased me," he wrote, "because at the time I had a strong conviction that the most effective photographic portrait is one that reveals the basic character of the subject in a state of repose, when the configurations of the face suggest identity and personality." Adams agreed with Stieglitz that much of the peculiar power of nineteenth-century portraiture derived from the static poses that were required for the long exposure time.

Leaves, Mills College, Oakland, California (c. 1932), Ansel's first close-up of a detail from nature, was in the batch that Ansel initially showed to Stieglitz. Just as the Transcendentalists were able to see the whole of nature in the smallest particle, the ravishing close-up of leaves captures the rhythmic orchestration present in all of the natural world. The leaves seem to emerge from an elemental darkness in an explosion of organic forms. The articulation of the long ferns that frame the composition has a musical quality.

Ansel recalled showing the picture to the dean of Yale's art department, who testily asked whether it was an etching, a lithograph, or a detailed painting. It took some doing to convince the dean that it was a photo taken directly from nature. Stieglitz's championing of photography as an art form may seem a commonplace today, when there are whole museums such as the International Center of Photography dedicated to the medium, but this anecdote is indicative of photography's low status, even in academia, at the time.

In a 1932 article for The Sierra Club Bulletin, Ansel championed the importance of close-ups in nature photography, with a line of analysis befitting other American Transcendentalists such as Henry David Thoreau or Ralph Waldo Emerson. He decried the modernist love affair with images of maximum size and effect, whether of people or places, and instead looked to the beauty that permeates all existence, from the grandest to the most minute of things. His feelings are directly in line with John Muir, who wrote, "When we try to pick out anything by itself, we find it hitched to everything else in the universe."

Adams understood that Americans appreciate a spectacle, but he pointedly quoted lines from the great American poet Walt Whitman: "These with the rest, one and all, are to me miracles/The whole referring, yet each distant and in its place." Whitman could almost be talking about an Adams photo here, with Ansel's technique of objectifying a scene into its component black, white, and gray tones, yet always revealing the interconnectedness of nature.

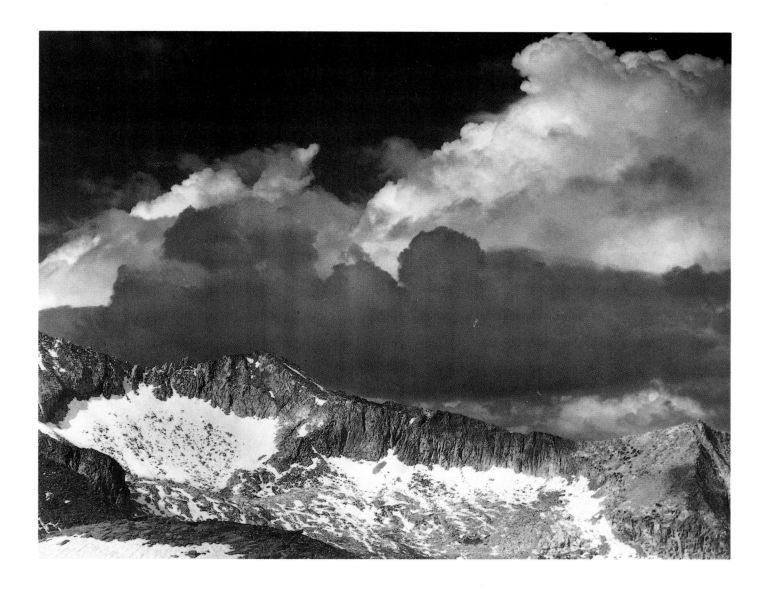

Muir, too, could be describing the feelings evoked by Ansel's photographs when he wrote of the Yosemite landscape: "Beautiful and impressive contrasts meet you everywhere, the colors of the tree and flower, rock and sky, light and shade, strength and frailty, endurance and evanescence." The dynamic tension between transcendental subject matter and modernist technique would reverberate throughout all of Adams' work.

In the wall-label for his Delphic Gallery show, Adams boldly declared, "Photography finds an admirable environment in the West. It is a new art in a new land."

Clouds—White Pass

The intent of this series of images taken in the 1920s and 1930s was to lobby in Congress for the creation of the Kings River Canyon National Park, which was officially designated in 1940. The dramatic, blackened sky and the great swath of dark cloud in the midground of this image set off the sharp details of rock and snow.

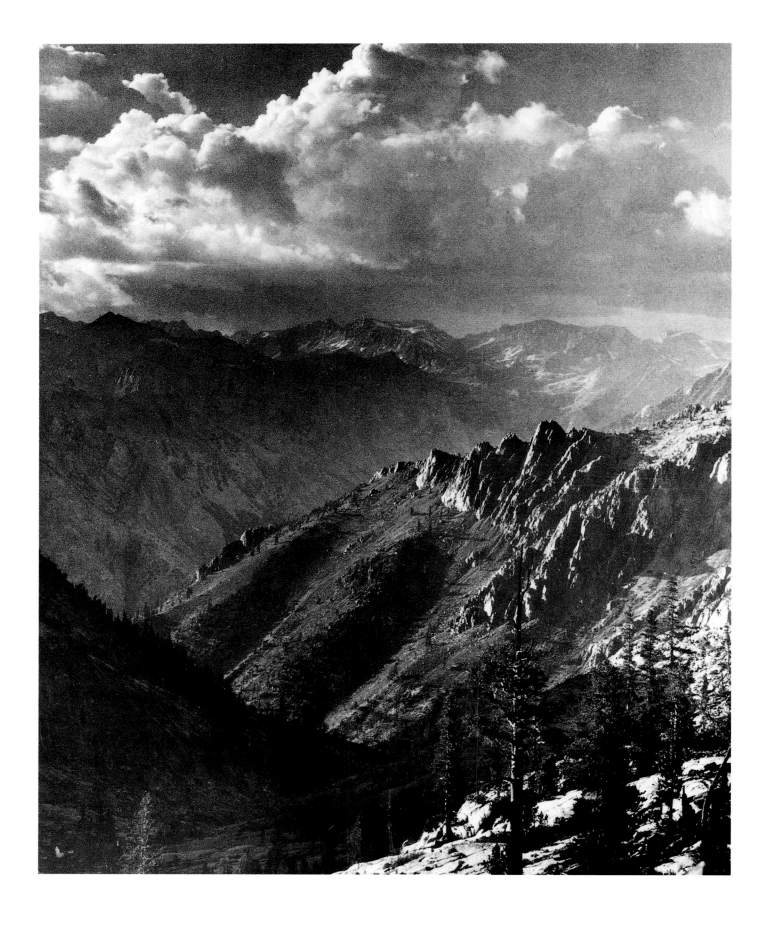

Paradise Valley

This is quite simply an Edenic view of the unspoiled western wilderness. The richly un-folding valley reveals a vision of bountiful and ever-replenishing nature. Adams gained his most widespread popularity for this beneficent vision of the wilderness, a trait he shares with the American Transcendental writers and the painters of the Hudson River Valley school.

Middle Fork at Kings River from South Fork of Cartridge Creek

Adams was always interested in more than just recording the scene around him, although this was a vital function of the Kings River Canyon series. The composition of this image expresses his transcendent view of nature, from the dominating tall pine to the varied shades of the valley and the low-lying clouds.

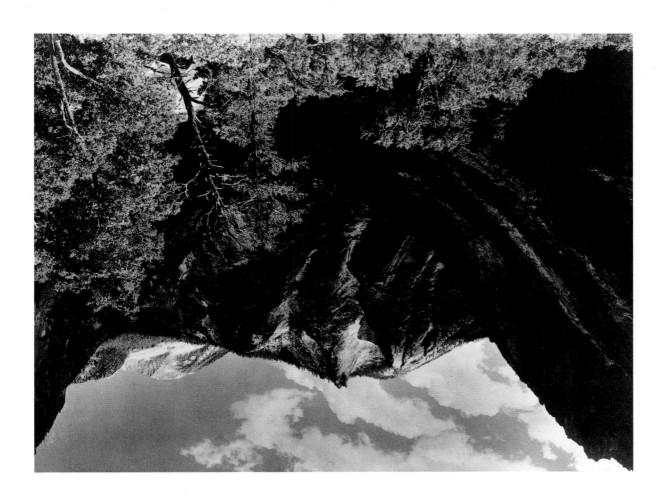

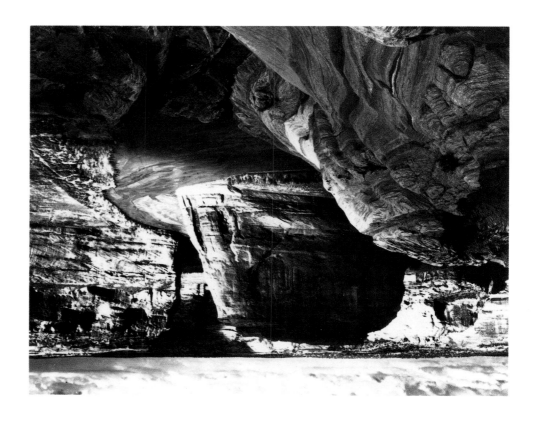

Canyon de Chelly

This image exemplifies the unity of style and subject that is characteristic of all of Adams' greatest work. Here, the "third dimension of mood," as he referred to it, is fully operative. The eye is drawn right to the highlight of the prowlike edge of stone against water, and then explores the sinuous course of the river—the same course by which the river has eroded its bed into the canyon. It is a timeless moment in an eternal process.

Canyon de Chelly

Adams took this image at almost the same time of day and year, and from a similar vantage point, that Timothy H. O'Sullivan took his in 1873. The images are subtly different, in part because of the different color sensitivities of the film stock used by each photographer. O'Sullivan's early film stock was more sensitive to the light from red rock, so the striations of "desert varnish" weathering are more subtly rendered. The focus of interest in Ansel's shot is the crisp contrast of the white dwelling against the deep black recess.

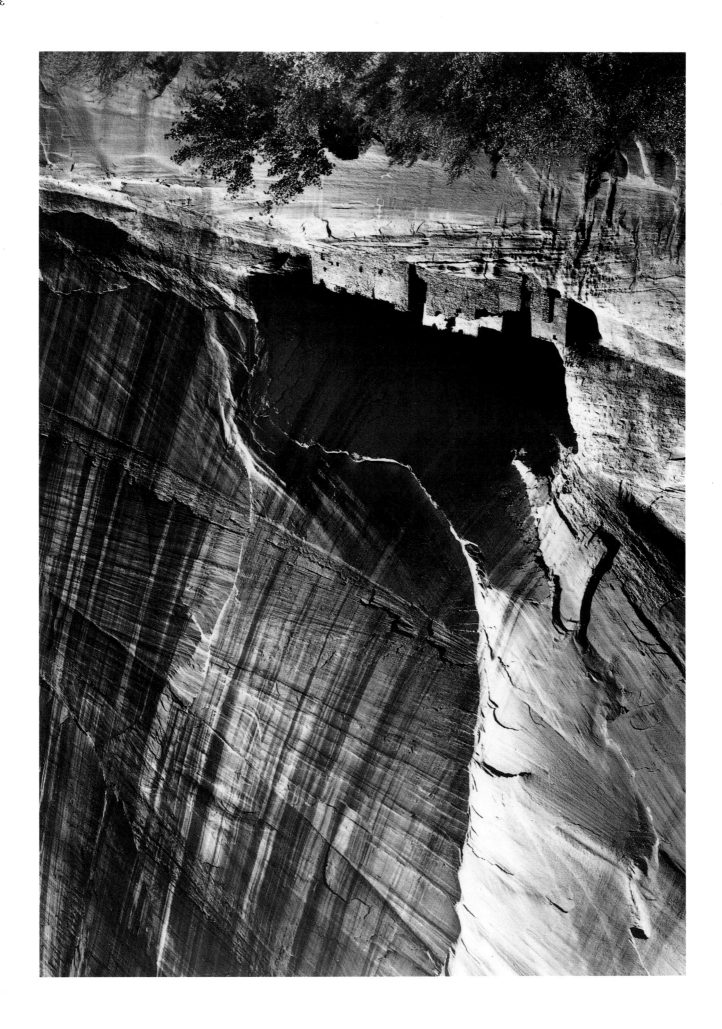

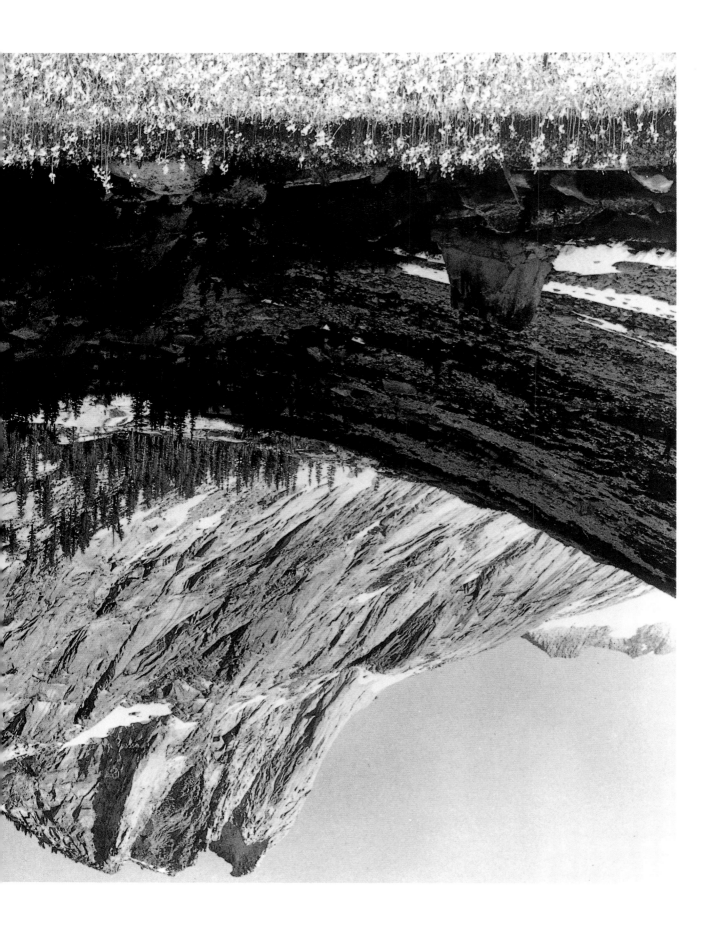

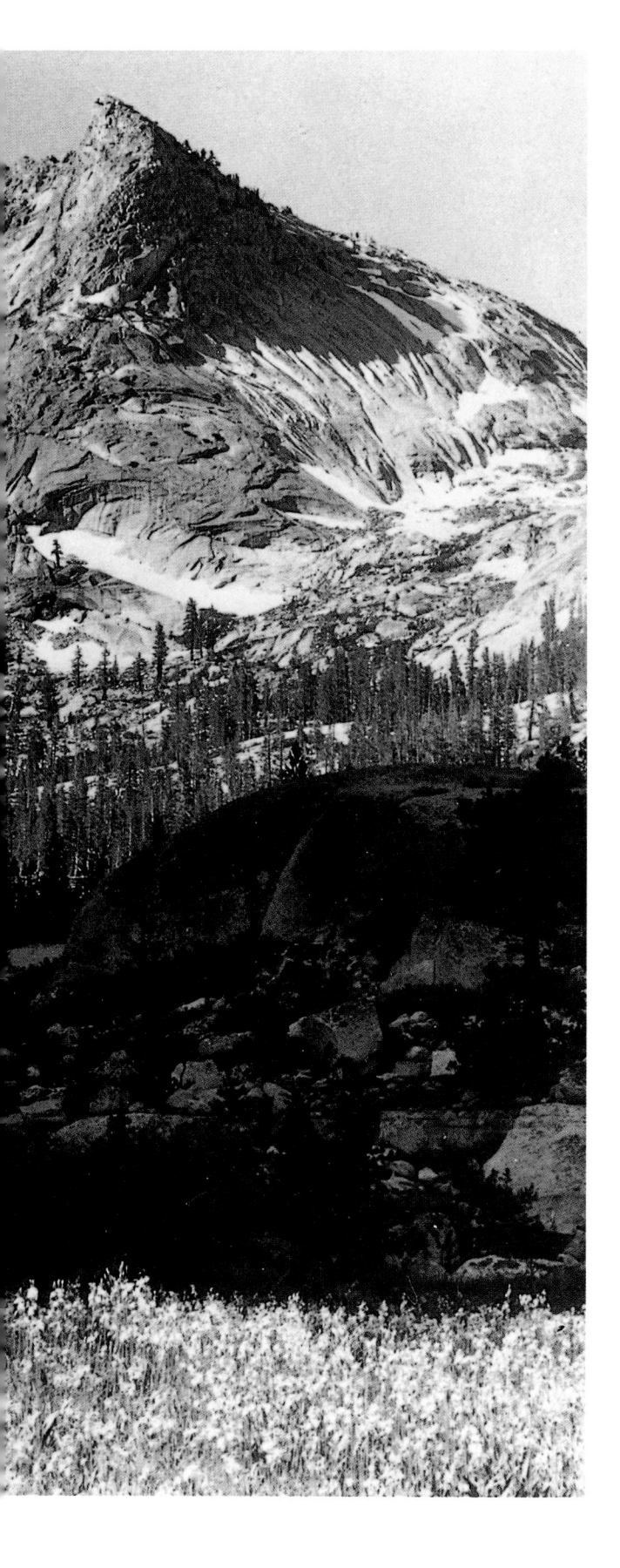

Boaring River, Kings Region

This placid image shows the contrasting emotions that Ansel was able to evoke from the Kings River Canyon, from the power of his rock studies to gentler images such as this one of nature in quiet harmony. Here, everything has its place, from the fragile plant stalks in the foreground to the pine making inroads on the rock face and finally to the austere cliffs towering over all.

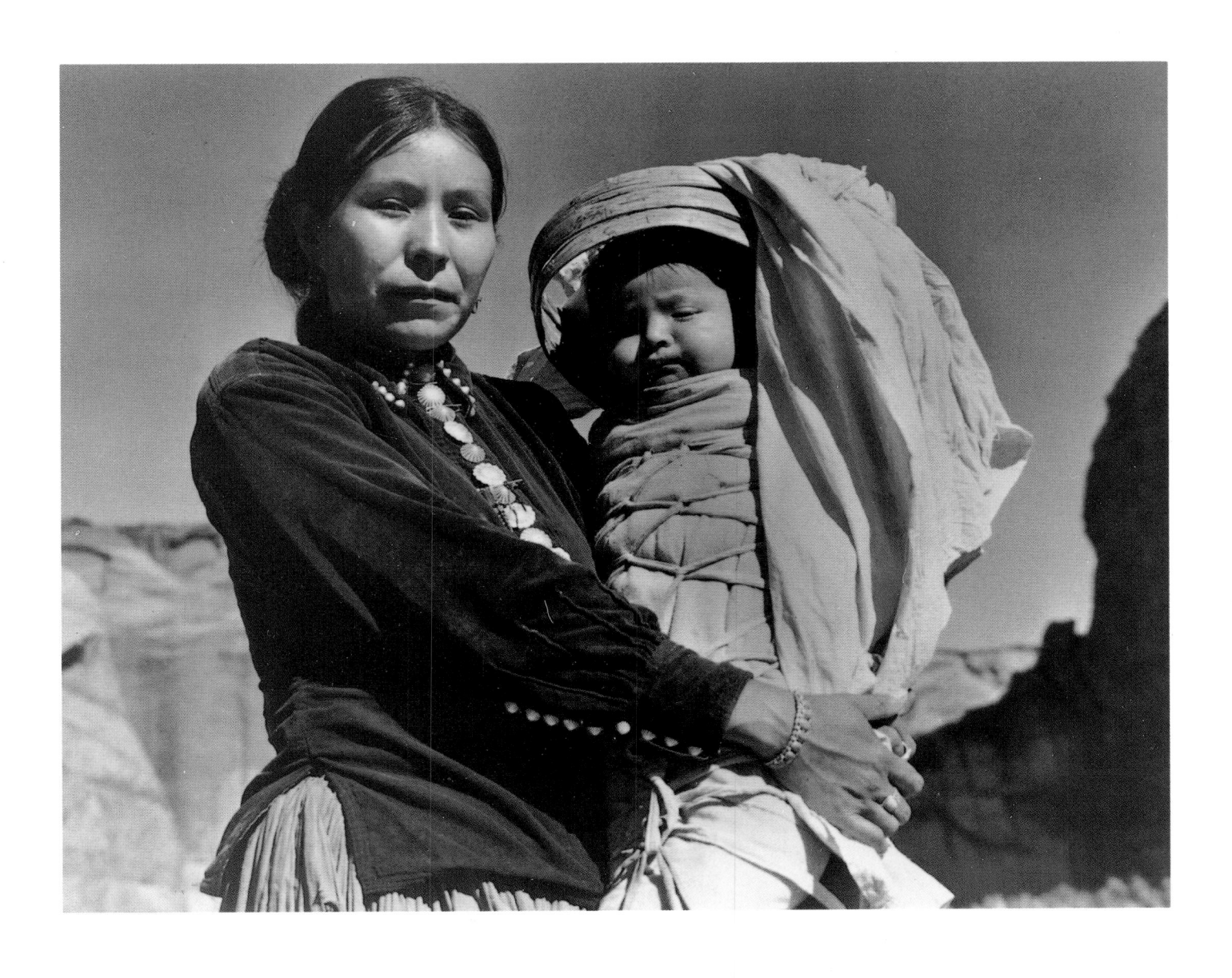

Navajo Woman and Infant, Canyon de Chelly, Arizona
Adams is not known primarily as a portrait photographer, and these images of Navajo Indians
living on land administered by the Department of the Interior are something of an anomaly
in his work. Ansel's style was to give his human subjects a monumental style, almost as if they
were objects in a landscape. The still pose and the angle from below emphasize this effect.

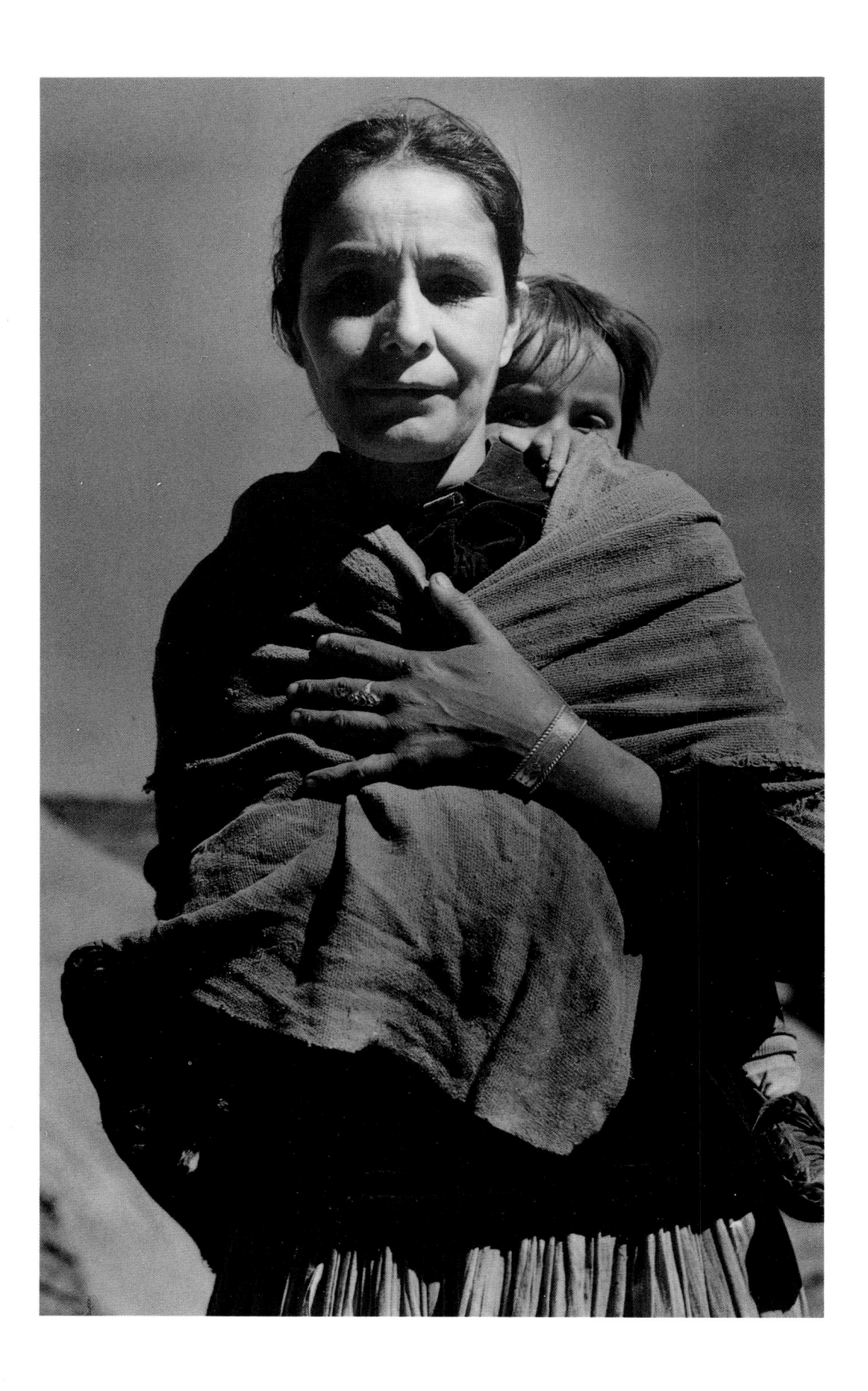

Navajo Woman and Child, Canyon de Chelly, Arizona
Ansel perceived the Navajo as an idealized example of people living in harmony with nature. This is another monumental treatment of its subject, with still figures posed against an empty sky so that the figures are presented as belonging, in the deepest sense, to the landscape.

35

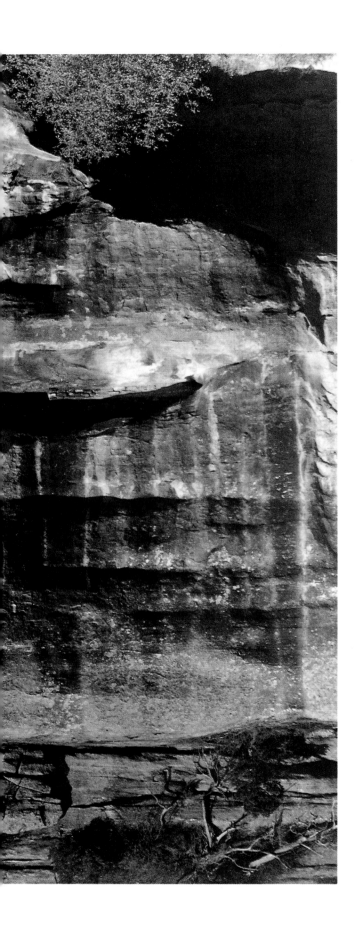

Mesa Verde National Park

The integration of civilization into nature in this image is juxtaposed with the endurance of the natural setting over the transient presence of man. The fragile-looking ladder in midground seems overpowered by the massive, streaked rock above, although the stone and wood technology is in complete harmony with the environment. Contrast the feelings of this image (taken in 1941) with Adams' mighty Hoover Dam series.

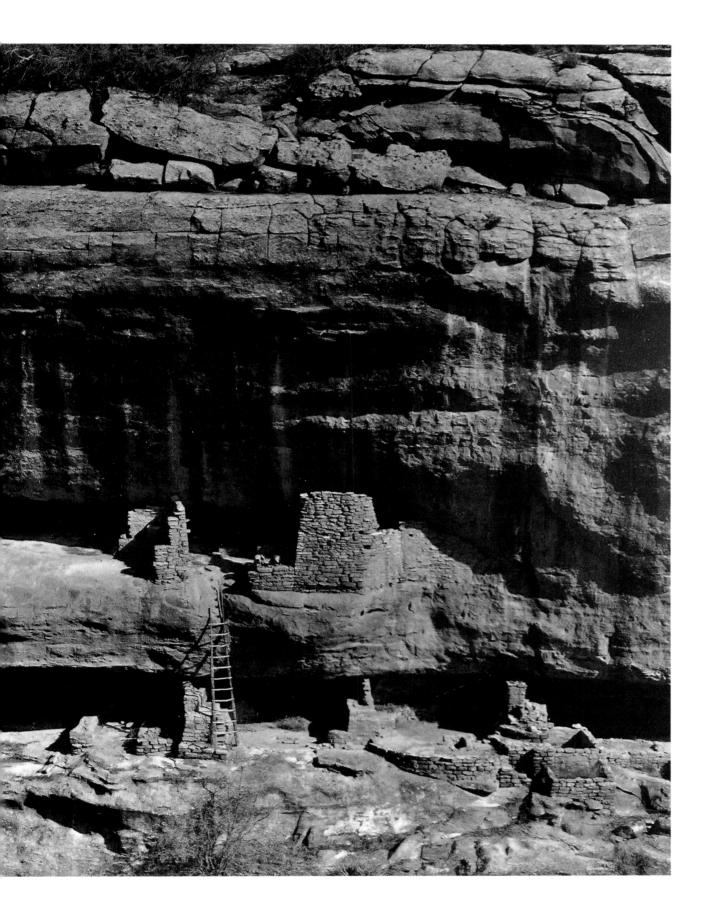

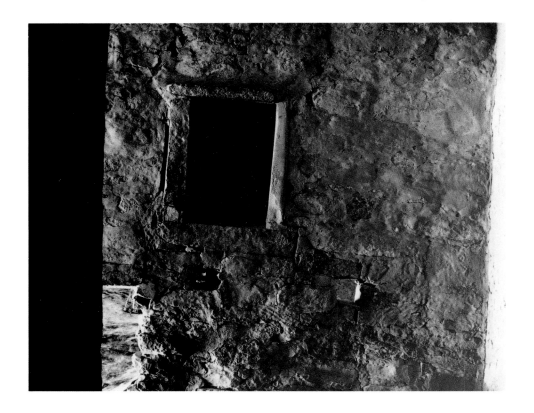

Interior at Ruin Cliff Palace, Mesa Verde National Park
This image (taken in 1941) is as much a study in pure forms and tonalities as a straightforward depiction of the site. The forceful black oblong to the left and the dark, empty window frames give the space a mysterious quality, while the lighter shades at the top and to the right complement the rectangular form of the composition.

Cliff Palace, Mesa Verde National Park
Texture and tonality are the focus in this image. The emphasis on the cracked quality of the surface of the walls makes the dwelling appear like a natural formation. At the same time, the deep black holes of the windows give the building a deserted, haunted feel. The Anasazi Indians were forced to abandon their structures in 1200 A.D. because of severe drought.

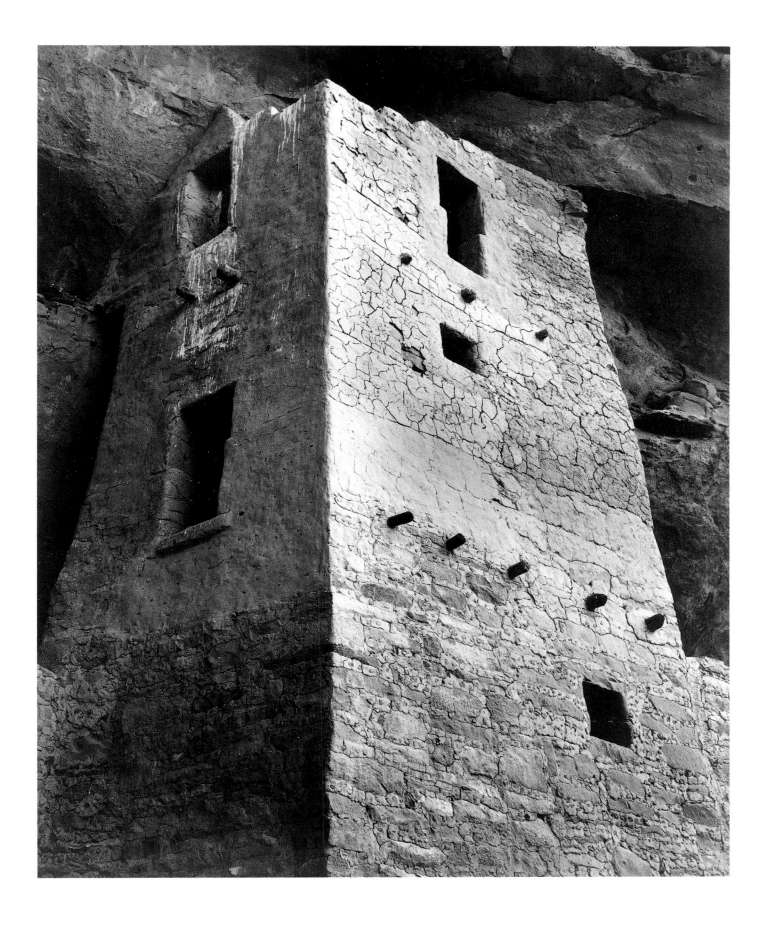

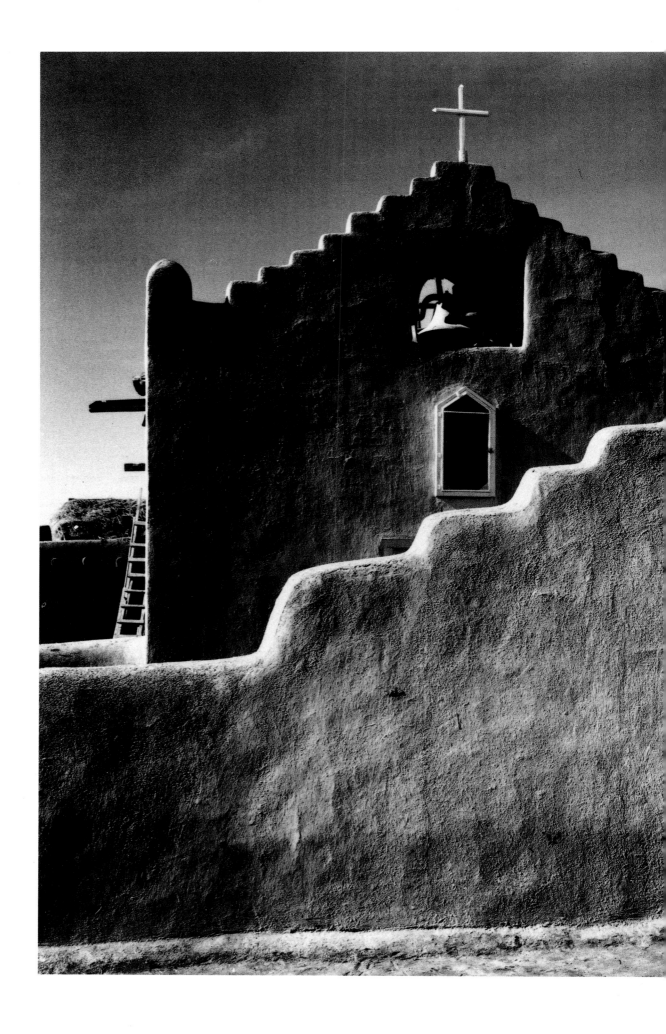

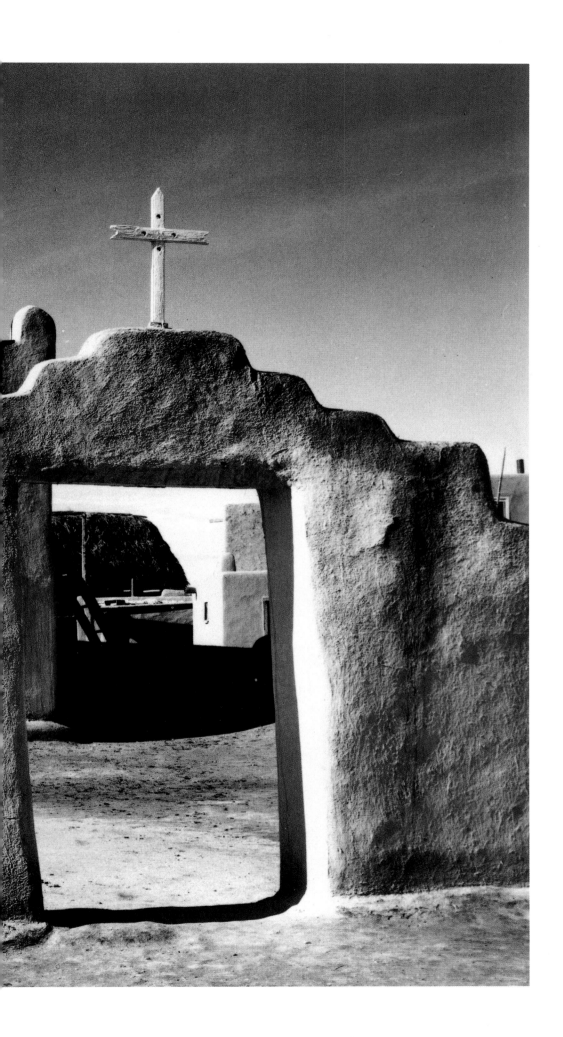

Church, Taos Pueblo, New Mexico

This wonderfully inviting image from 1941 shows the care that Ansel took in placing his camera to form his composition. With only a slight shift in position from the vertical image on the following page, the composition is opened up so that the eye follows the highlights on the step-shaped walls up to the plain wooden crosses.

41

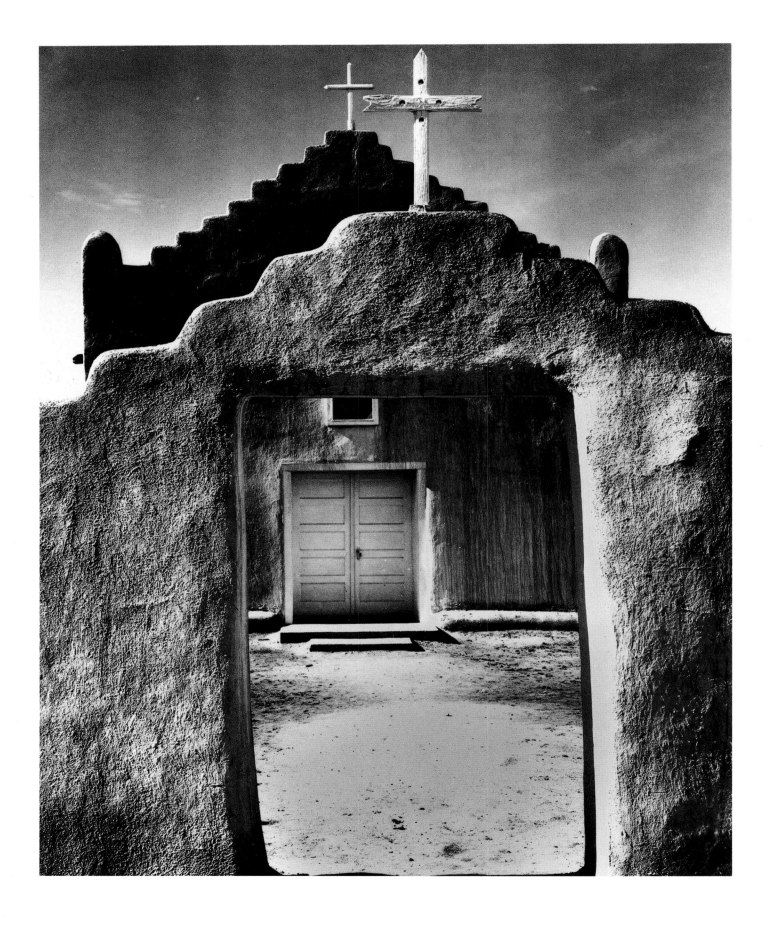

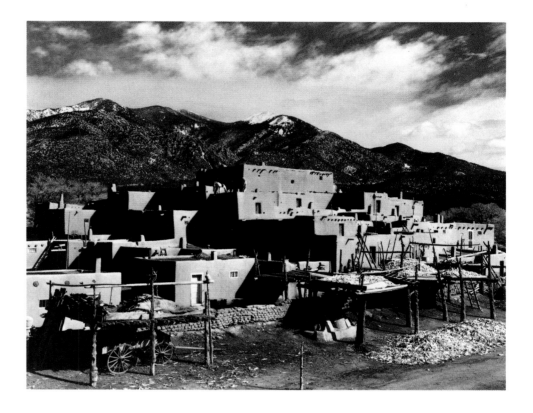

Taos Pueblo, New Mexico

A bold use of deep black shadows makes the building seem subservient to the natural setting yet at the same time something distinctly apart from it, with flat, gray planes and right angles that appear nowhere else in nature. The shadows in this image, taken in 1941, make these contemporary dwellings seem as deserted as the ruins of Mesa Verde.

Church, Taos Pueblo, New Mexico

Adams' predilection for clean edges, well-defined forms, strong contrasts, and varied tones is evident in this photo from 1942. The composition of rectangles within rectangles is surmounted by the step formation of the walls, in both cases highlighted against a darker background. The highlighted crosses recall his famous image *Moonrise, Hernandez*, showing that he was always on the lookout for natural manifestations of his interior beliefs, rather than merely being at the right place and time with a shutter.

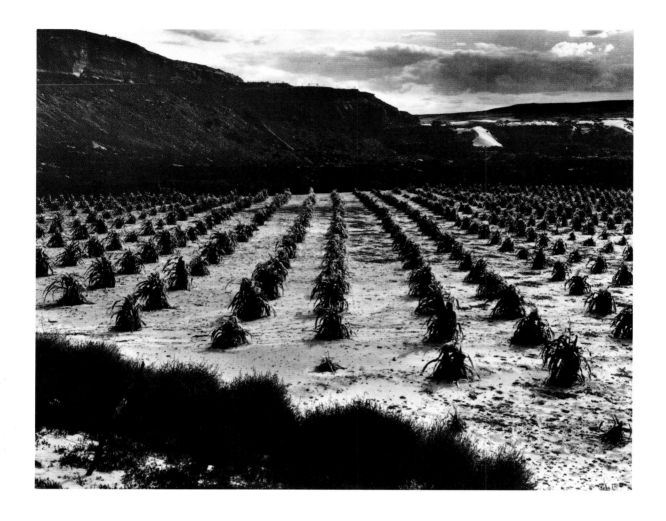

Corn Field, Indian Farm near Tuba City, Arizona, in Rain

Orderly rows of somewhat bedraggled-looking corn stalks in the rain on a sandy field stand
out against the encroaching wilderness as seen in the vivid black thicket in the foreground.
Agriculture is seen at once as part of nature and in defiance of it in this image from 1941.

At Taos Pueblo

Nature, always foremost in Adams' vision, here seems more vibrant in the solid black outlines of the tree trunks than do the evanescent works of man, which almost look as if they could fade into the mists of the background. Once again, there is no sign of a human presence.

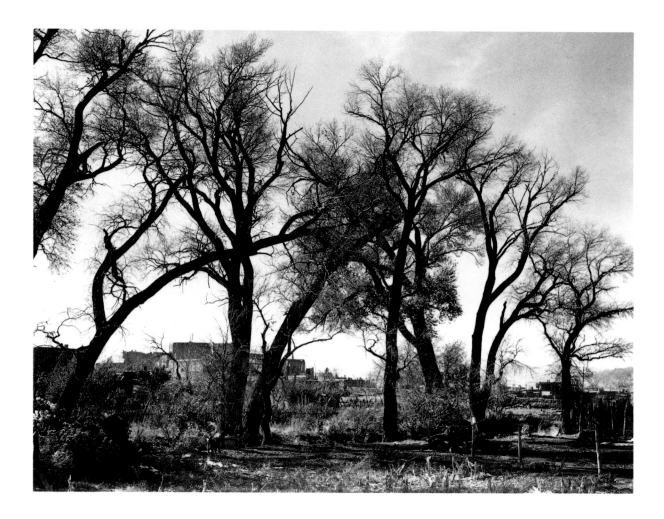

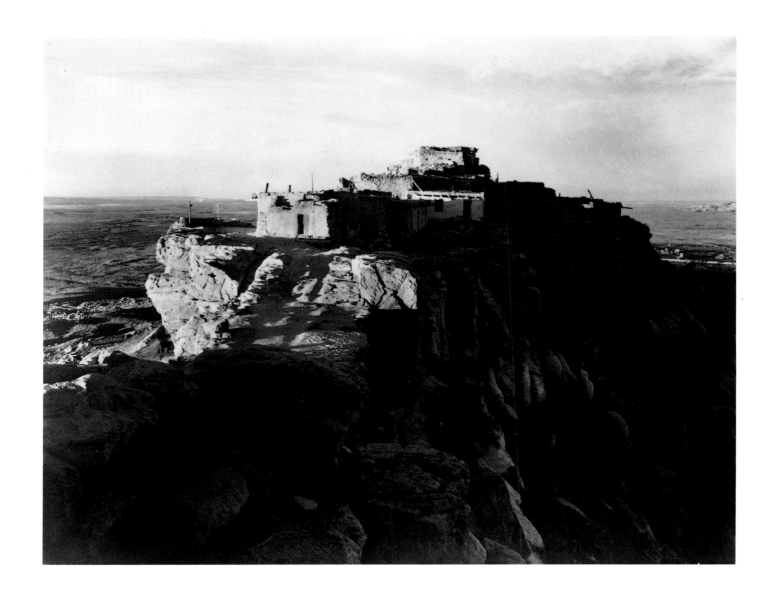

Walpi, Arizona

In comparison to the following photograph, this image, also from 1941,
reveals more of the foreground and is exposed to show more detail in the
texture of the rocky promontory. Combined with the softening sunshine on the
doorway, the overall effect is to integrate the building into its environment.

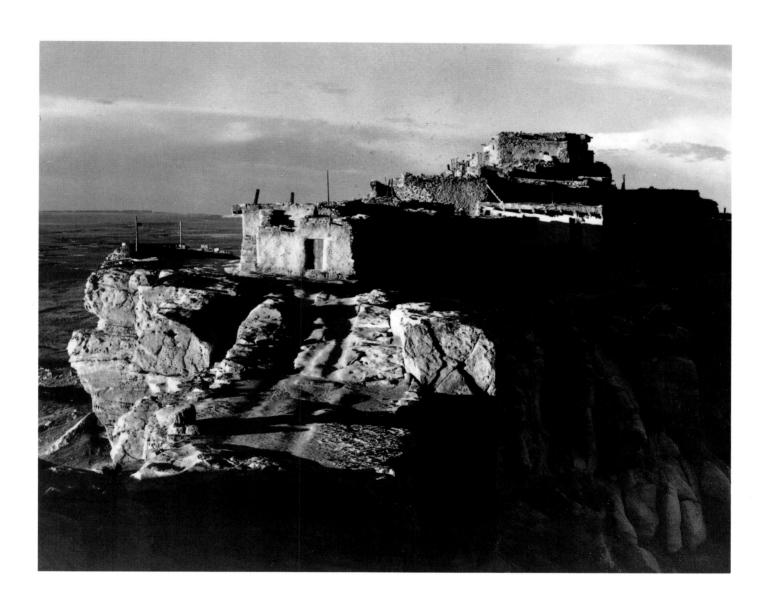

Walpi, Arizona

Ansel's understanding of how subtle changes in composition and exposure can profoundly alter the emotional expression of a picture can be seen by comparing this image with that of the preceding one. This close-up view (taken in 1941) emphasizes the stark quality of the structures rising out of deep shadow

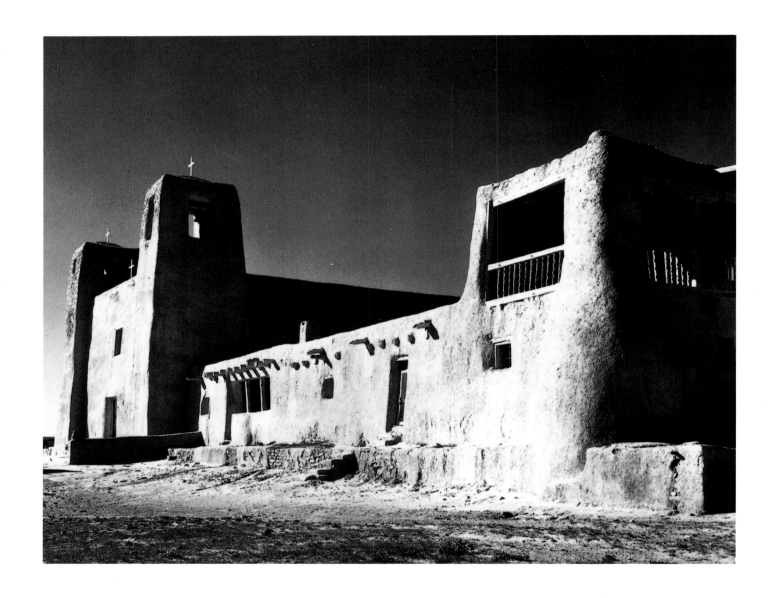

Church, Acoma Pueblo

This image is vibrant with the contrasts of a thoroughly modernist technique
applied to an ancient subject. The building is expressed in pure forms of shadow
and tone against a dark sky. The eye follows the breathtakingly clean edges
of the highlighted wall against the shadows up to the luminescent crosses.

CHAPTER TWO

THE RANGE OF LIGHT

The World of Work

In January 1934, Ansel was beginning to codify his photographic technique in a series of articles for the journal *Camera Craft*. He shied away from calling his method "pure" or "straight" photography, because he did not want to speak for other practitioners, such as Weston, Strand, and Stieglitz. In his first article he defined a critical duality of photography: it is an expressive form entirely dependent on technical means. "In no other form of art is technique more closely interwoven than in photography," Ansel wrote. "The photographer who thoroughly understands his medium visualizes his subject as thing-in-itself. He visualizes, before operating the shutter, the completed photography." Ansel felt that mastery of technique would only free up the artist to more fully express himself.

He also addressed the complexities and contradictions of photographing landscapes. Landscapes offered some of the most challenging conditions in photography because the photographer frequently has little control over his point of view to compose the shot, and must deal with uncontrolled light sources and extreme ranges of light and dark, along with the weather. Again, Adams stressed that the feelings and aesthetic ideas that are evoked supersede the mere recording or prettifying of the scene. Great technical skills are needed to photograph landscapes but without this basic aesthetic and spiritual understanding, the result is only pretty postcards, something Ansel felt had impeded the progress of photography as an art form.

Critics who dismiss Adams as a mere technician or nature photographer miss this essential element of aesthetic choice made in each stage of the process. For Ansel the photograph was never simply about recording nature, or showing off technical proficiency, but rather combining both to express an emotional state.

Perhaps this was part of the problem Ansel had in reconciling his creative photography with the work he did to make a living. Unlike contemporary photographers such as Irving Penn and Bruce Weber, Adams made a sharp distinction between the two. Part of the reason may have been that he had to master a technology that was new and by nature somewhat alien to him: artificial lighting for interior photography. In the 1920s, interior lighting had not progressed much beyond the nineteenth century.

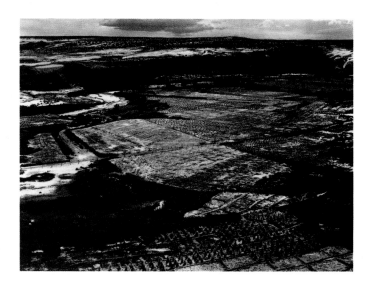

Corn Field, Indian Farm near Tuba City, Arizona, in Rain
This high aerial shot (from 1941) is a clear example of the aesthetics of so-called straight photography as professed by Adams and the other members of Group f/64. Everything in the panoramic scene is in sharp focus, from the pines in the foreground to the stubbled corn and distant trees, forming a quiltlike texture.

Dutifully, Ansel purchased the state-of-the-art equipment of the day: a flash gun, black powder cap detonators, and magnesium flash powder. The pyrotechnics were reasonably safe, he concluded, as long as the ignition was far enough away from one's eyes. The proper exposure was determined by referring to an index—again, a method against the grain of Ansel's instinctive style.

Ansel's very first commercial photographic assignment in 1920 couldn't have been more contrary to his preferences for style and subject matter: he was hired to take a picture of a roomful of six-year-olds at the Chinese Baptist Kindergarten in San Francisco! Inadvertently, Ansel set out many times the amount of flash powder required. He raised the flash gun, made classic look-at-the-birdie noises to attract the attention of the youngsters, and detonated his charge. The resulting lightning-and-thunder explosion knocked him to the ground. When he got up to look through the lens, everyone was gone. The chil-

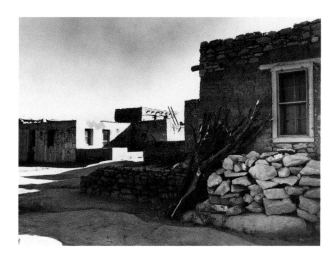

Acoma Pueblo

Ansel's ambivalent feelings about the presence of humans in the landscape are revealed in this image. The buildings are seen as an extension of nature in the pile of rocks and wood in the right foreground, but the stark shadows and bright sunlight in the background flatten and negate the human presence.

dren had all ducked under their desks and were beginning to cry, for the billowing smoke brought the fire department with sirens blaring.

Ultimately, Ansel finished the shot in the playground, in more conducive outdoor lighting. In the rather humble-looking print, his subjects peer out morosely, perhaps fearing another explosion. The framing of a long foreground and high background draws the eye to other elements of the picture: the mottled texture of the playground floor, the chalked-in hopscotch game, the vertical shadows of the fence, and the strangely trapezoidal form of the black gate. The children look a little like specimens captured in a man-made wilderness, perhaps a reflection of Ansel's own discomfort about his business situation. In another early shoot, for a wedding party, Ansel managed to burn the lintel of a doorway with his flash powder and ended up spending more for the repainting than he earned for his pictures.

In the lean years of the Depression, Ansel kept food on the table by shooting for catalogs and industrial reports and working in architectural photography and portraiture. His subjects included men's dressing gowns, cement workers, and a field full of turkeys. Fortunately, electric flash bulbs were in use by the time Ansel hung out his shingle as a professional photographer in 1930, although there were still a few bugs to be worked out in this regard. The bulbs were not yet protected with plastic safety coating and would explode unexpectedly. Once, it worked out to Ansel's advantage when he was taking a portrait of the British novelist Phyllis Bottom, whose mien was singularly inexpressive. A bursting flash bulb gave her some animation in subsequent exposures.

In his own mind, Ansel could never successfully reconcile the demands of the marketplace with his own need for inner expression. "The professional photographer," he wrote, "takes assignments from 'without,' injects what imagination he can apply, and does the best he can with the problems presented. The creative photographer, on the other hand, takes assignments from 'within' and, if truly dedicated, may find that the client is tough and uncompromising!"

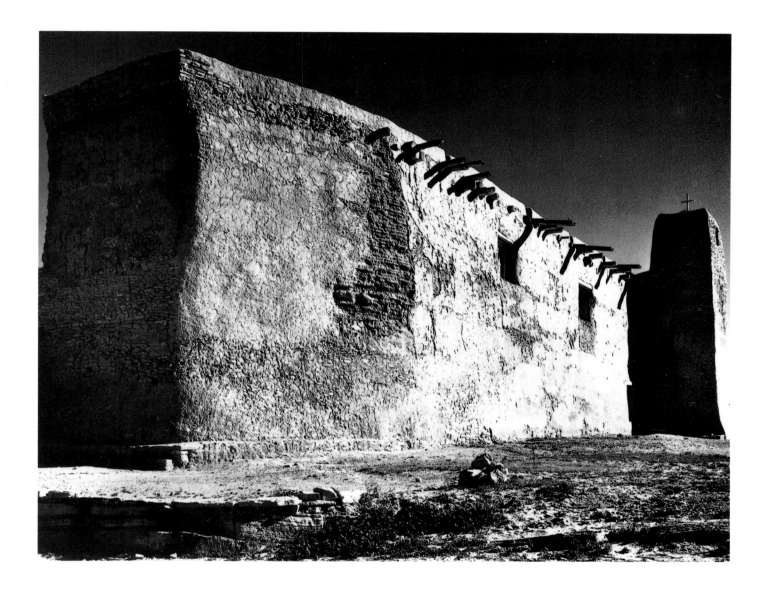

Personally, Ansel found the dichotomy between the demands of the "within" and "without" insoluble.

Perhaps the dilemma was too close to what Ansel felt was a basic misunderstanding about his work: that he simply captured images from nature, rather than interpreting them. In the documentary about him, Ansel uses very similar terms to describe his creative process: "When I'm ready to make a photograph, I think I quite obviously see in my mind something that is not literally there, in the true meaning of the word. I'm interested in expressing something which is built up from within, rather than just extracted from without." Commercial work, or even work with propaganda value, like much of the social realist photography in the 1930s, would always be too much "extracted from without" for Adams.

Church, Acoma Pueblo
When compared with Plate 33, this image shows the range of expression that can be drawn from the same subject by varying composition and exposure. Here, the emphasis is not so much on the edges of the forms but on the battered texture of the wall. The deep black oblongs to the left and right give the church a citadel-like quality.

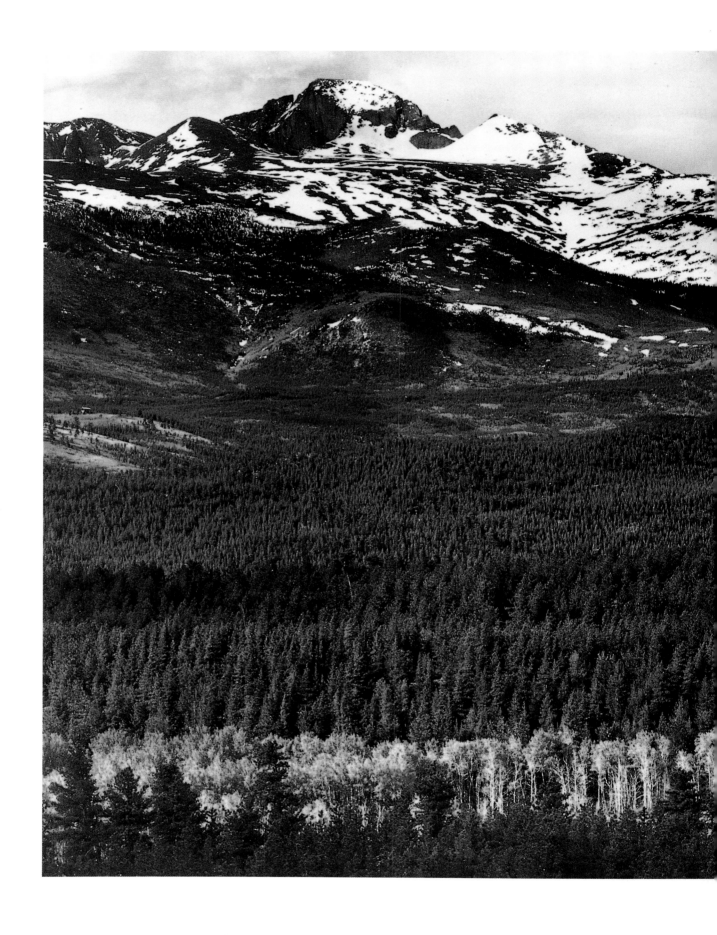

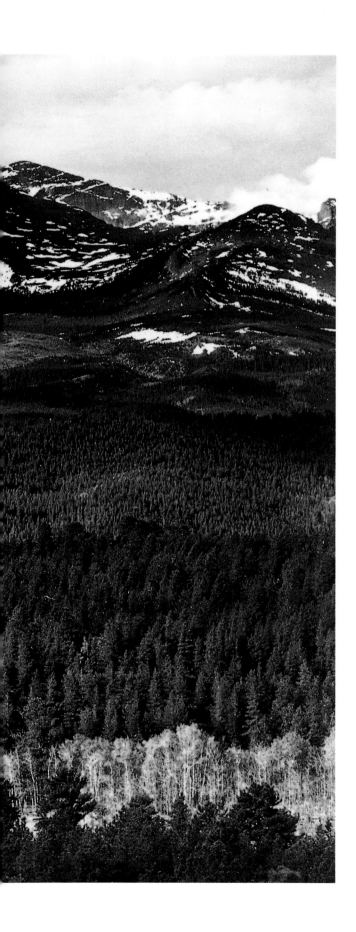

Advertising and Magazine Work

For someone with as exacting an eye as Ansel for the textures and forms of nature, advertising photography could be little more than a joke. He recalled setting up a composition for a client, a dried fruit company, to do a "compelling photograph of raisin bread." Ansel set up the shot, only to have the real raisin bread replaced with smooth-textured white bread to which raisins were added with tweezers. The bread was shellacked with a brownish liquid to give the illusion of a perfectly smooth raisin bread, such as could not be found in nature. Like most American products, it was better than the real thing. Ansel was especially surprised that the ad was meant to appear in a national bakers' journal, for the delectation of a readership who knew such texture was impossible. The studio experience was light years away from the sense of awe and delight Ansel felt in the presence of nature.

Field work was somewhat more congenial, but it was plain that Ansel did not have a great rapport with objects made by the hand of man. In 1945 *Fortune* magazine hired him to do a survey of all the architecture parlant buildings, like the Brown Derby restaurant in the shape of a hat. Ansel drove hundreds of miles in a relentless drizzle in search of what he called "architectural monstrosities" before the assignment was abandoned.

An interesting sidelight in Ansel's career was the giant Colorama slides produced for Eastman Kodak and displayed in the Grand Central Terminal in New York beginning in 1948. Ansel had been working in the giant, blow-up format from as early as 1935 when he was commissioned to do a series of 40-by-60-inch

Long's Peak from Road, Rocky Mountain National Park
Subtle gradations of tone are used to compose this image.
A dark line of trees makes up the lower border of the picture,
topped by a highlighted stand of trees. Modulating bands
of gray lead into the distance. The eye vaults across the
great space from the lighted trees to the distant snow fields.

wall murals for the San Diego Fair. Photomurals were quite a fad of the era, and could be found in bank lobbies, travel bureaus, and corporate waiting rooms. Ansel was fascinated by the technical challenge of resolving the delicate balance between tone and grain, the silver particles in the film. He concluded: "I would rather have a richness of tone and a little grain than no grain and an unsatisfactory tonal image."

The Colorama was a giant, 18-by-60-foot-long transparency mounted in front of a bank of fluorescent tubes above the concourse of Grand Central. Ansel felt the Coloramas were by and large "aesthetically inconsequential but technically remarkable." The transparencies often showed two subjects taking pictures in a landscape proportioned for Cinemascope; Ansel had used his photographic assistants Don Worth and Gerry Sharpe as models.

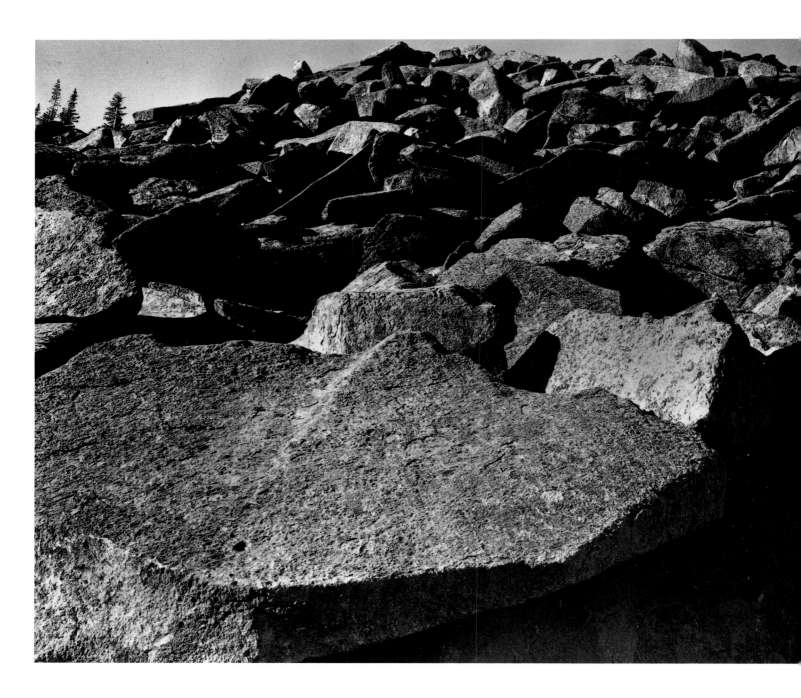

The Making of Aspens

Ansel took two of his best-known black-and-white photographs while he was scouting around in New Mexico for a new Colorama image. The two prints, both called *Aspens, Northern New Mexico* (1958), were taken within an hour of each other on a clear and windless fall day. Ansel recalled spotting the stand of young aspens with mellow golden leaves in the Sangre de Cristo Mountains north of Santa Fe. The trunks of the aspens were tinged with green and the leaves were a glowing yellow against a ground of rust-colored shrubs. In fact, the setting was ideal for color. But it was just this kind of simple-minded color "scenery" photograph that Adams deplored. He felt that what was visually interesting at some level did not necessarily convey an important feeling.

He set to work with his 8-by-10 camera, a 19-inch Cooke lens, and—a surprising choice for any other photographer—black-and-white Kodak Panatomic-X film. Knowing that normal exposure and development would produce a flat, grayish image, Ansel chose a deep yellow Wratten No. 15 filter to reduce the shaded background values and heighten the contrast of the trees, lit by ambient light from a blue sky. It was fortunate there was no wind because of the long, one-second exposure time to compensate for the filter.

He first took the horizontal picture with the glittering leaves on the young tree, and then the vertical image with the sharply defined highlights on the tree trunks. In *Examples,* Ansel wrote that the Aspens photos worked at all levels of appreciation but that "I do not consider them 'pretty' scenes; for me they are cool and aloof and rather stately." A color picture would have been muted, with darkly shining

Moraine, Rocky Mountain National Park

Fully half of this image is dominated by the texture of the large rock in the foreground. The photo has something of the Transcendentalist philosophy to it, in that the entire nature of the rock field is contained in a single stone. Deep black shadows and thin highlights define the rugged quality of the glacial deposit.

In Rocky Mountain National Park

An intensely darkened sky provides this image with a delightful symmetry between the patches of bright snow on the black earth and the white clouds against the black sky. Alternating tones of gray in the different cloud strata create a musical dialogue between heaven and earth.

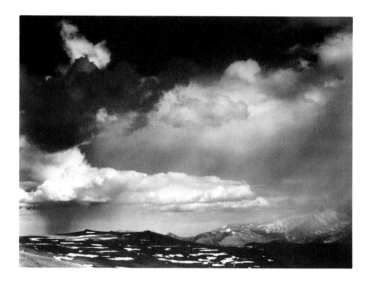

hues; Ansel's choices in black and white brought out a bold, full range of hues.

In Adams' hands, what would have been a photographic staple of autumn leaves instead becomes something much more complex and rich. The two aspen tree photos express something more timeless about the life-giving nature of light itself. It is sunlight that seems to draw these frail-looking, beautiful young trees out of the void. In the horizontal shot, the smallest of the trees stands in vibrant glory before the dark woods, full of young life and energy. The leaves in the photo become important not for their pretty colors but for their capacity to catch the light, just as they are important in this way for the tree. Yet this is not a spring scene but an autumn one, leading to the long dark of winter. The picture

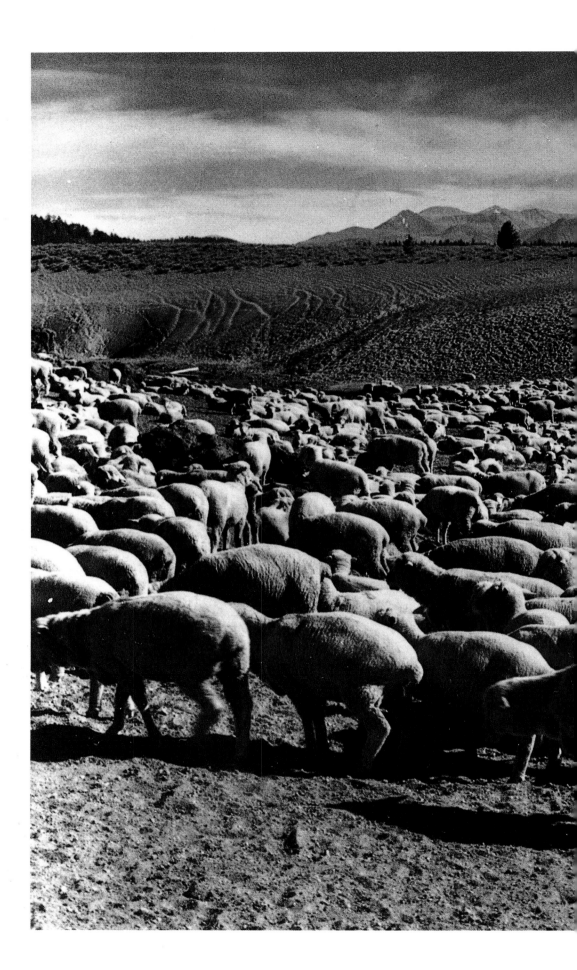

**Flock in Owens Valley,
California**

This uncharacteristic shot
(from 1941) of livestock in
the landscape has more of a
spur-of-the-moment, docu-
mentary feel than Adams'
formally composed mountain
shots—no doubt because
of the shifting nature of the
subject! Ansel was plainly
interested in recording all
aspects of the varied territo-
ries administered by the
Department of the Interior.

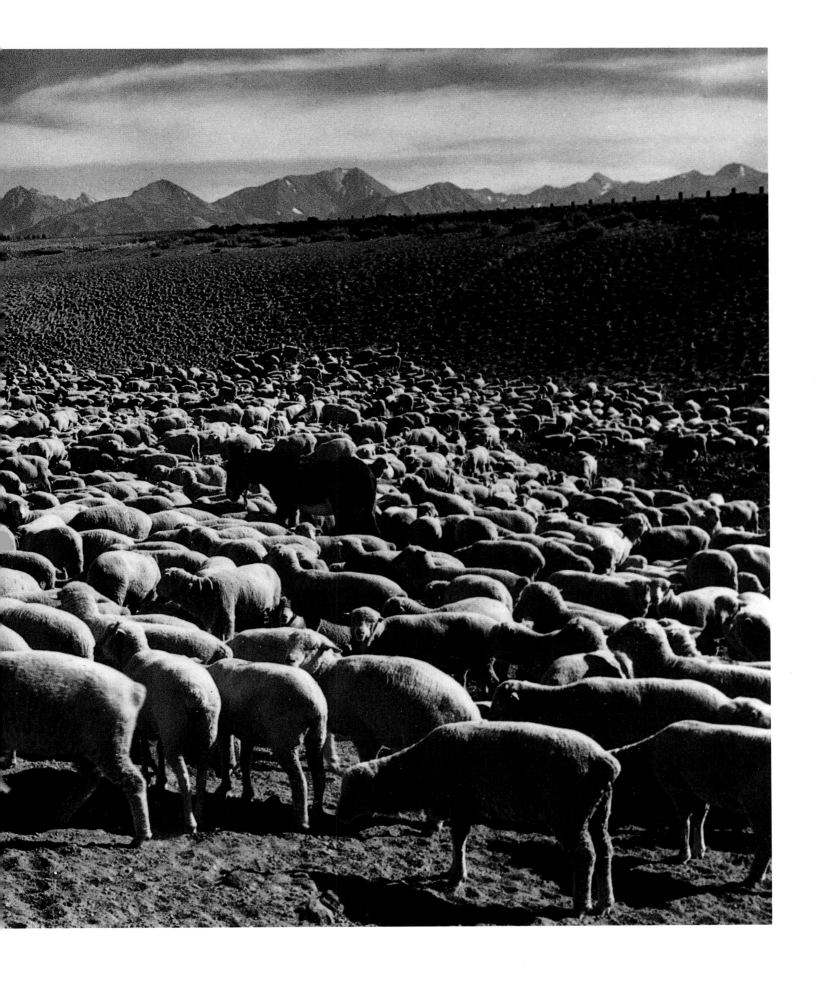

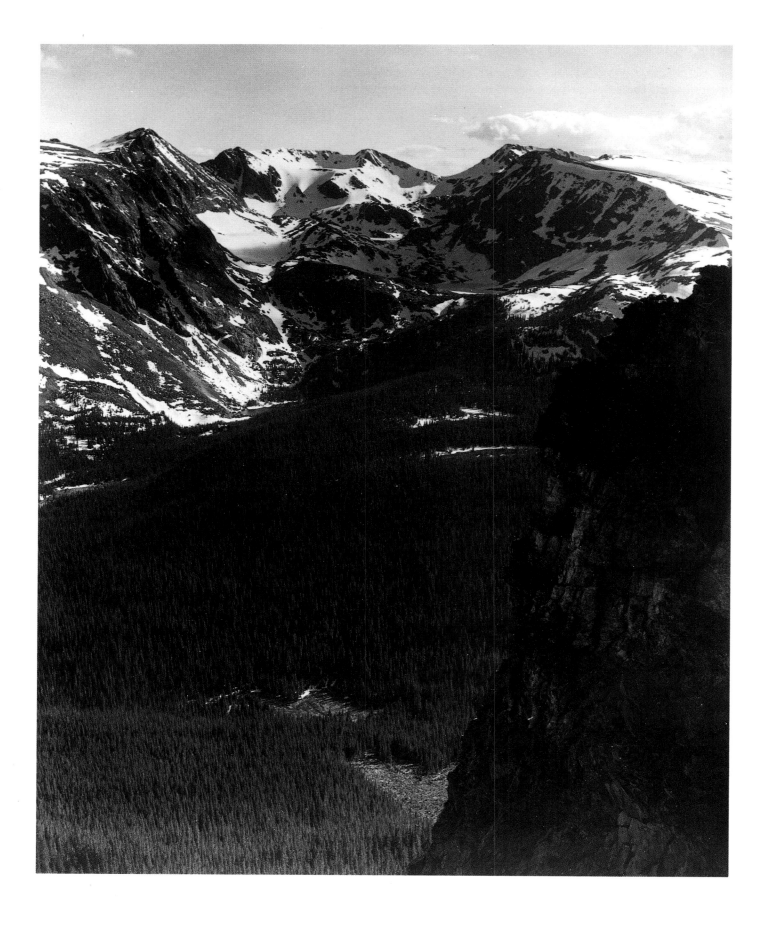

seems to vibrate back and forth in time: it can be seen either as young life emerging in the foreground, or the many-hued trees receding into darkness and oblivion.

As in many of Adams' greatest images, the moment of the photograph seems poised between two eternities, the renewal of life and the permanence of death. We contemplate one brief, shining moment, the life of a young tree at the change of seasons. The vertical image is a more solemn procession of trees that seems to emerge from the darkness to experience the white highlight of the sunlight on their trunks. Ansel's choice of the yellow filter and higher than normal paper contrast forged this vision, because it was in reality not a sunlight scene. Ansel remarked that many people simply assumed the image was of sunlit leaves. He was constantly surprised that people presumed that a photograph was nothing more than a faithful copy of nature.

Ansel manipulated the highlights for very specific purposes: first for their beauty as objects in and of themselves, with the alternating patterns of white, black, and tonal vertical bands, and then for the emotional resonance of the thin, bright lines against the black background. The razor-thin presence of the light is the reason the trees can exist. The coming darkness is experienced with a kind of awe and terror.

Ansel would have discounted such intellectualizing about his images, although he would not have discounted the emotional content. For him, the emotion of a photo as conveyed by the technique was always primary. He wrote his biographer Nancy

In Rocky Mountain National Park
Some of Ansel's most serene images of nature in the parks series were taken in Rocky Mountain National Park. Here he found an affinity with his beloved Yosemite. This is a marvelously ordered image, with thick stands of trees in the foreground, still snow fields, and the silently passing shadow of a cloud.

Newhall about one of his pictures, "Like it but can't yak about it." But his letters reveal how seriously he considered the subject matter of his work.

In 1947 he wrote a letter to Eldrige T. Spencer, president of the San Francisco Art Association, that spoke directly to the creation of such images as Aspens. Adams stated that great art had something to do with life in the time to come, not just in the present, and that nature for him represented many things, but above all a sense of limitless potential.

"The relatively few authentic creators of our time possess a resonance with eternity," he wrote. "I think this resonance is something to fight for—and it takes tremendous energy and sacrifice." In the same letter, Ansel shows how out of step he was with other currents of modernist thinking, particularly the content of anxiety, or despair, about the human condition. Even though his photos were on the cutting edge of defining a thoroughly modern, clean-edged "straight" photography, Ansel's thinking belonged in a sense to an earlier era—upbeat, relentlessly positive, hopeful about the human condition.

He had little patience for the exploration of the pathological that became a keynote of art in the mid-twentieth century. Even the popular insistence on political importance and social meaning in the documentary photography movement in the 1930s could cause him to use an uncharacteristic expletive. His Transcendentalist leanings were misunderstood by other modernists, who saw his views as corny, sentimental, or, most unforgivably, belonging to the past.

Like Frank Lloyd Wright, Adams found himself in a somewhat anomalous situation. He was a fountainhead of modernist technique but his Transcendentalist philosophy was no longer in keeping with the times. Thus he was regarded in some critical circles as a bit of a dinosaur. For his part, Ansel denounced the soullessness in modern art, just as Wright faulted the sterility of the Internationalist movement in architecture. Both men sought to utilize modern means to express timeless truths.

Figures in a Landscape

Ansel's Coloramas for Grand Central were a horse of a different color. The Coloramas, because they were promotions to encourage people to use Kodak film, necessarily had to include people in them. But Ansel was never quite comfortable integrating figures in a landscape. The human presence somehow seemed to diminish rather than enhance the scale of what he felt about nature. Even in black and white, the pose of the cowboy in *Horseman on Pohono Trail, Valley Rim, Yosemite Park* (c. 1930s) is so hopelessly sentimental that you almost expect him to start yodeling. The young lovers gazing rapturously over a mountain range for a cover Ansel did for *The Argonaut* look as posed as any Maxfield Parrish subject.

Perhaps Adams just did not have the same perception for the eternal and the sublime in the human figure as he had for the natural world. As a result his Colorama images are somewhat of a mixed bag, with the sophisticated horizontal composition of the landscapes and the almost hilariously kitschy human figures amidst the scenic splendors. His Colorama #69 shows an all-American Dad posing with a fish in his net for Mom, who is snapping the picture, and a boy and girl. Weirdly, mother and children, are also posed artificially on a dead stump. In Colorama #157, another unit of Americans poses incongruously at Zabriskie Point in Death Valley, which the Italian film director Michelangelo Antonioni used as an objective correlative for American alienation in his film called, naturally, *Zabriskie Point.*

In all of the above situations, the posing of the subjects is sentimental. The feeling conveyed is not genuine and this jars with the Transcendentalist nature of Adams' true subject matter. The emotional power of Ansel's work flows from the connection he makes with the viewer, particularly in communicating his sense of awe and unfolding joy in nature. A stand-in subject in the frame only intrudes upon this relationship. Ansel reveals where his aesthetic heart lies

In Rocky Mountain National Park

Tall, highlighted trees are outlined against a massive black triangle in the lower half of this image. The eye is then led across contrasting tones of gray to the light value of the plain in the midground and the softly defined hills in the background.

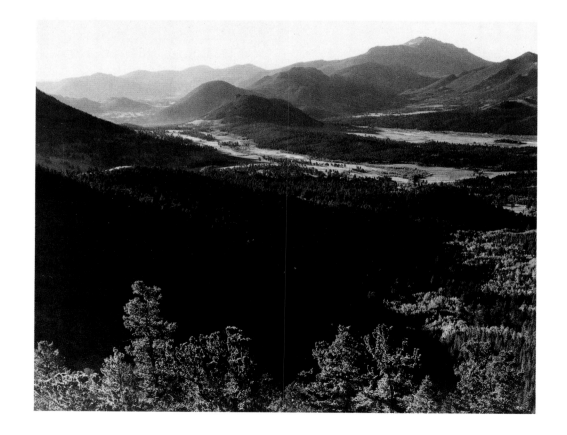

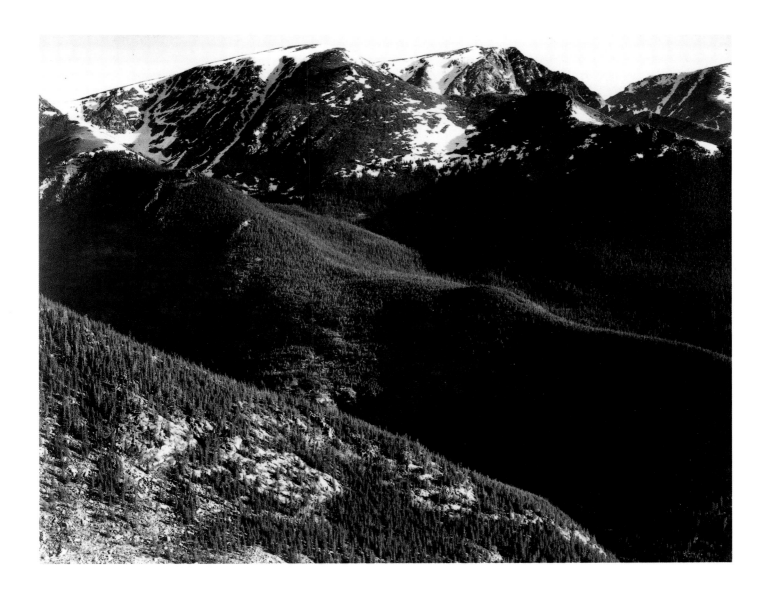

in the 1981 documentary film as he walks through Yosemite and says in appreciation, "When you look down to Yosemite Valley, you can't see a single work of man."

The photographer made two other forays into the commercial world, both of which earned him stern rebukes from his good friend, photographer Imogen Cunningham. In 1969, for one of his last commercial jobs, Ansel allowed the Hills Brothers company to reproduce his photograph *Yosemite Valley, Winter, Yosemite National Park* on a coffee can, surely one of the more unusual photographic collectibles. "The image had a certain dignity,"

In Rocky Mountain National Park
This is a stately, ordered image in which the downward slopes in the foreground and midground play off against the snowy cliffs and border of gray sky. The eye is drawn deep into the composition across undulating ridges.

Ansel concluded. "Potentially corny: actually reasonable." Then when Ansel did a television ad for Datsun in 1973 that showed him next to one of their cars working on a photo of a forest, Cunningham railed at him, "Adams, you've sold out again!" The advertising campaign did have a conservation theme, however; for every person who test-drove a Datsun, the U.S. Forest Service planted a tree.

That was Ansel's last endorsement of a commercial product. His summation of these experiences shows his deep commitment to the environment: "I have been offered extravagant sums of money with the intention that *Winter Sunrise* be splashed across magazine pages and billboards on behalf of a whiskey. I choose instead to have images reproduced on behalf of the cause I believe in: creative photography and environmental protection."

The Best of Friends

Ansel's growing friendship with Beaumont and Nancy Newhall in the late 1930s was more important to him than any commercial venture. Beaumont was a Harvard-trained art historian and one of the first champions of an art-historical approach to the neglected medium of photography. His wife Nancy Newhall would write the first important retrospective of Adams' work, *Ansel Adams: The Eloquent Light*, published by the Sierra Club in 1963.

Adams first encountered the name Beaumont Newhall while reading a rather harsh review in the January 1935 issue of *American Magazine of Art* of a piece Ansel had written. Ansel believed he was a neophyte in the rarefied world of museums and art, and agreed that his Group f/64 Manifesto may have been a bit strident but that it probably would not have been as effective otherwise.

Ansel's lifelong association with the Newhalls would provide an entrée into the world of fine art. He heard

In Rocky Mountain National Park

This plate is a good example of the daring, formalist elements almost hidden in many of Ansel's images. On one level it is a straightforward rendition of a sunny promontory in front of deep shadow; but take notice of the pure, clean edge between black and gray and the amazing conjunction of pure white, deep black, and gray planes in the center of the picture.

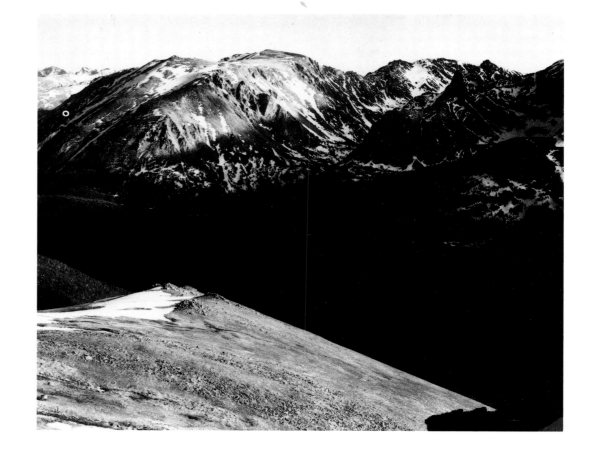

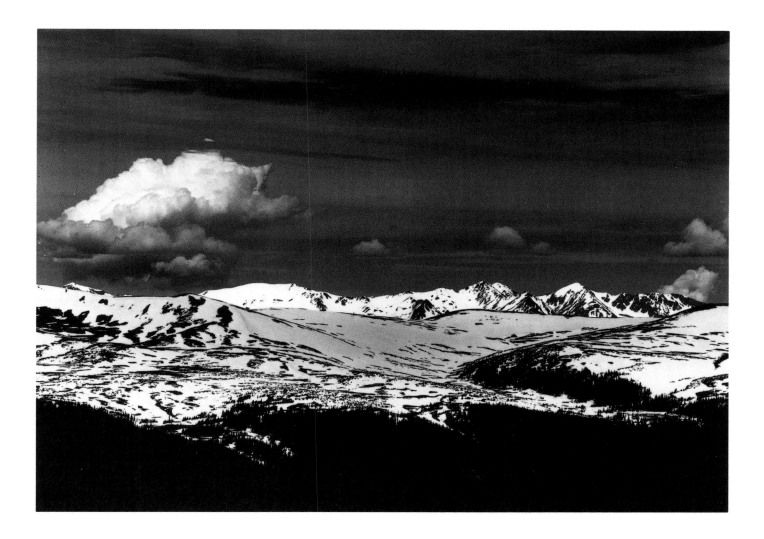

again from Beaumont Newhall after the publication of the first of Adams' technical books, *Making a Photograph*, later that year. Beaumont sent him a warmly effusive letter, and the two began a correspondence. They met for the first time in front of the Museum of Modern Art in New York in 1939. Nancy Newhall recalled the incongruous appearance of the mountaineer on the streets of New York, delighted with a new tripod: "Now, black hat tugged firmly down, with his mountaineer's loping stride, he was clunking the tripod along the pavement. At the corner of Fifth Avenue we waited for the light to change. People stopped to look at him better: some tittered. For a moment he looked sad and a little severe, then he lifted his chin, smiled and we went clunk! clunk! across Fifth Avenue to our favorite Cafe St. Denis."

Rocky Mountain National Park, Never Summer Range

This image has the marvelous, etched quality of a photographic negative. The black swath of trees in the foreground is exposed and printed just enough to show texture against pure white snow fields. The edges between light and dark are wonderfully detailed, from the spiky tops of the evergreens to the cool white profile of the mountain against a gray sky.

The Art of the West

The Newhalls made their first visit to California to see Ansel and the show he'd curated, "A Pageant of Photography," for the Golden Gate Exposition in San Francisco in 1940. Ansel chose an eclectic mix of images to display the range of photography from its beginnings to the present day, from landscapes by Timothy H. O'Sullivan to Man Ray's "Rayographs."

O'Sullivan, who took photographs of the Southwest in the 1870s, was a personal favorite of Ansel's. Adams' *White House Ruin, Canyon de Chelly National Monument, Arizona* (1942), is in many respects a tribute to O'Sullivan's masterful *Canyon de Chelly, Arizona*, from 1873. Ansel raved that the show contained some of the best images that he had ever seen. The hefty catalog included criticism by Edward Weston, Maholy-Nagy, Dorothea Lange, Beaumont Newhall, and others.

Ansel took the Newhalls to the Top of the Mark for drinks and a view of fog rolling in over the bay. Nancy later wrote, "By far the finest art we saw in the West was in photography, not in painting, nor sculpture, not even in architecture. Beyond question, photography was the art of the West."

Ansel then drove them down to Carmel to meet Edward Weston, which resulted in Nancy editing Weston's personal journals as the *Daybooks* volumes, published in the 1960s. Adams took some of his most purely abstract images in the series *Surf Sequence, San Mateo County Coast, California* (1940) along the Pacific Coast Highway 1. The images have that quality of spontaneousness combined with a rigorous craft that is so distinctive of Adams' work.

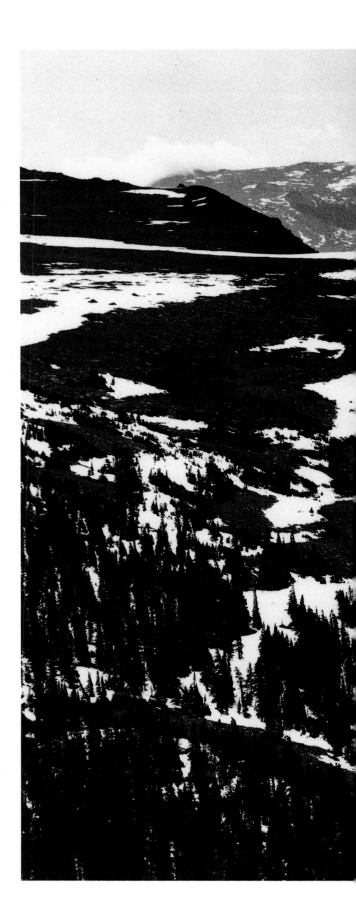

Long's Peak, Rocky Mountain National Park

Trained as a classical pianist, Ansel often used musical metaphors while discussing his photography. This image has a distinctly fugal quality in its sense of diminishing scale, from the tall pines in the foreground to the smaller versions in the midground and the barely discernible trees at the border of the dark foothills near the gray mountain. A continuation of the theme is implied far into the background.

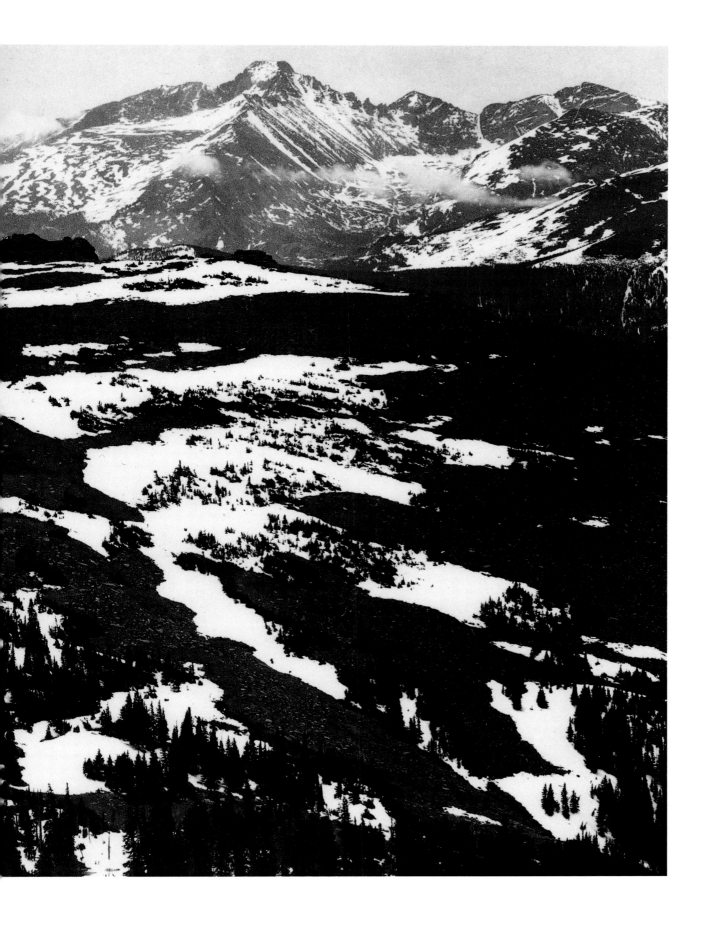

The excitement of discovering a beautiful found object is part of the appeal of his photos. Ansel pointed the lens of his 4-by-5 view camera straight down from the top of the cliff to the patterns of surf forming and reforming on the wet sand below. Fascinated by the ever-changing values of sunlight and water, Ansel clicked off shot after shot.

He immediately envisioned the exposures as a group. Ansel knew that, to work as a series, the photos would require an overall tonal balance, but this did not turn out to be simply a matter of developing them all the same way. The sun had shifted in the twenty minutes or so that it took to make all the exposures so the overall luminance value was different, making each negative a bit more exposed and somewhat denser than the one preceding it. The value of the sand in the midground changed from shot to shot too, depending on how wet the sand was.

He resolved the problem with a lot of judicious dodging and burning, hand manipulating the tonal intensities of the print in the darkroom. This is another example of the aesthetic interpretation of reality that Ansel used to give an illusion of effortless spontaneity. This almost invisible technique combined with the eye of an artist is what gives Adams' pictures such depth.

The photos are so strong because they work both as natural images and as abstract forms of brilliant

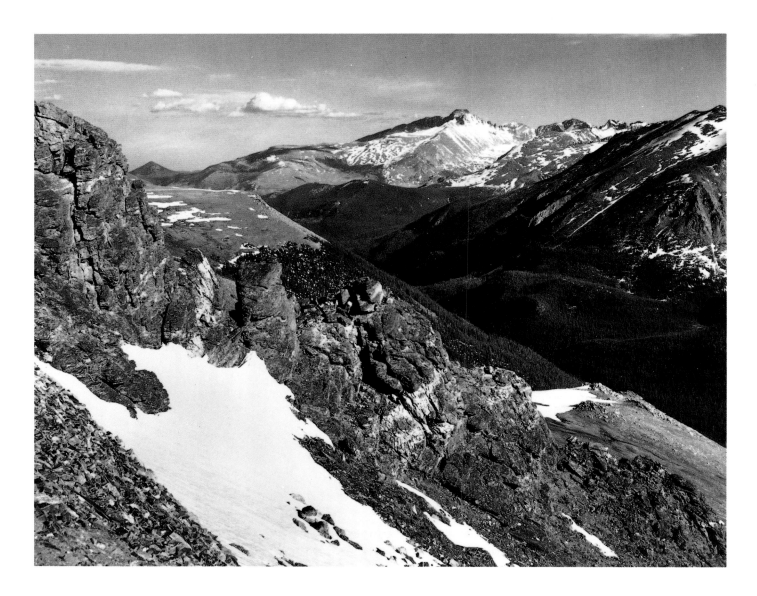

whites, lustrous grays, and deep blacks. We can almost hear the soft sizzle of foam on porous sand as the eye traces the sinuous line of water. The process of erosion and change is nearly tangible even though, of course, we are looking at still images. A given frame could almost be a blow-up of a brushstroke, in the way that the painter Roy Lichtenstein would later magnify a single brushstroke with his dot matrix method.

Ansel had an uncanny eye for seeing the world as a pure object. He quoted his friend, the photographer Minor White, saying that "a sequence of several images can be thought of as a single statement."

Photography and the Museum of Modern Art

Photography got a much-needed boost in self-esteem as a field of art from the actions of Beaumont Newhall in 1940, who helped found, along with David McCalpin, the Department of Photography at New York's Museum of Modern Art. Adams was on board from the very beginning as a committee member. In a piece for the book *Miniature Camera Work* in 1938, Ansel had waxed visionary in a review of a show curated by Newhall for the Modern:

> **Whoever saw the recent Exhibition of Photography 1839–1937 at the Museum of Modern Art in New York could not fail to realize the true meaning and attainments of the art. . . . Photography is the most potent, the most direct, the most stimulating medium of human expression in this day. Call it Art, term it Craft, place it with journalism, science, physics or self-expression, it is not to be denied. Never in all history has such an instrument of Kaleidoscopic powers been placed in the hands of men for the dissemination of thought,**

Long's Pass, Rocky Mountain National Park
Adams was never afraid to make bold use of startling zones of pure white and deep black. This plate is exposed and printed so that the detail in the snow field is burned away to create an intense, abstract white form in the foreground. The eye travels easily from the white void to the richly detailed peaks in the background.

In Rocky Mountain National Park
The shapes of passing clouds are echoed in bright patches of snow on the mountainside, creating a symmetrical composition. The viewer is drawn to look deep into the frame, to the far black ridges against a gray sky. A further symmetry is created by the near black triangle on the right, below a gray cloud mass.

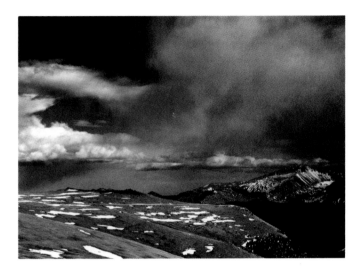

> **fact, and emotion. . . . Photography is doing for the modern age what the early printing presses did for the post-Renaissance social expansion.**

Adams and Newhall thought it important for Stieglitz to join them because he had been for so long a lone voice in the wilderness proclaiming photography an art. Stieglitz's refusal was phrased in his customary blend of cordiality and cantankerousness: "My Dear Adams: I have nothing against the Museum of Modern Art except one thing & that is that politics & the social set-up come before all else. It may have to be that way in order to run an institution. But I refuse to believe it. . . . In short the Museum has really no standard whatever." Stieglitz concluded the letter, "But it's good for me to know that there is Ansel Adams loose somewhere in this world of ours . . ."

Nancy Newhall, who had an insider's knowledge of the chill between her husband and Stieglitz, later

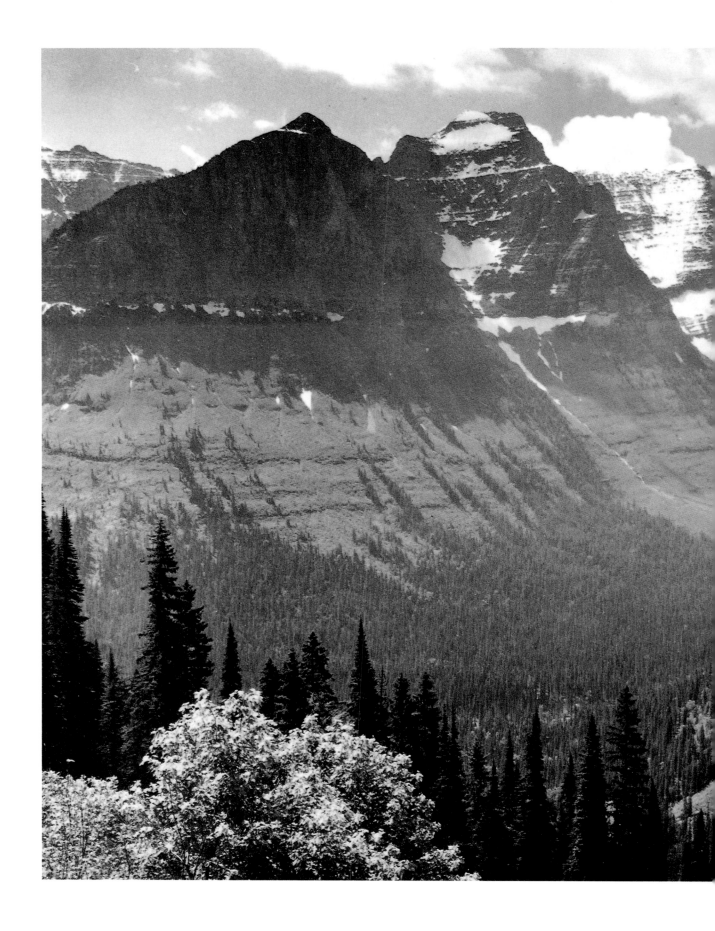

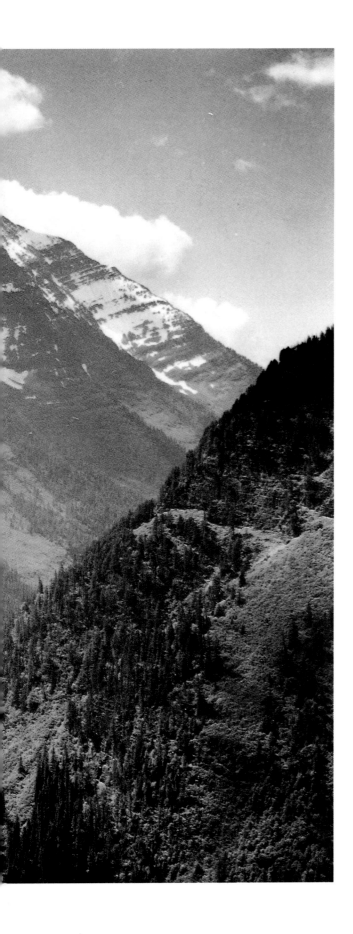

concluded, "It was years before [Beaumont] realized that Stieglitz expressly had founded An American Place to counteract, so far as he could, the intellectual exhibitionism of the Museum of Modern Art."

Ansel and Beaumont curated the first show of the museum's photography department, "Sixty Photographs," which opened on December 31, 1940, and featured works dating from the 1840s up to contemporary works by Adams and Weston. Stieglitz, too, was represented. The show was a resounding "who's who" of creative photographers since the very beginnings of the medium, including Mathew Brady, Berenice Abbott, Eugène Atget, Henri Cartier-Bresson, Walker Evans, Laszlo Moholy-Nagy, Man Ray, Charles Sheeler, Edward Steichen, Edward Weston, Clarence White, Stieglitz, and Adams.

Newhall's vision of the purpose and direction of photography was in complete synch with Adams' beliefs of modern technique combined with a spiritual or transcendental content. In his book *The History of Photography*, Newhall concluded:

> **More and more are turning to photography as a medium of expression as well as communication. The leavening of aesthetic approaches which we have noted continues. While it is too soon to define the characteristic of the photographic style of today, one common denominator, rooted in tradition, seems in the ascendancy: the direct use of the camera for what it can do best, and that is the revelation, interpretation, and discovery of the world of man and of nature. The greatest challenge to the photographer is to express the inner significance through the outward form.**

In Glacier National Park

This is an exhilarating example of the varied terrain within our national parks. A highlighted, leafy tree stands in bright relief against a dark line of pines descending into the valley. Light gray patches define the limits of the tree line in midground, and bright snow drifts make a vivid contrast with dark rock faces in the background.

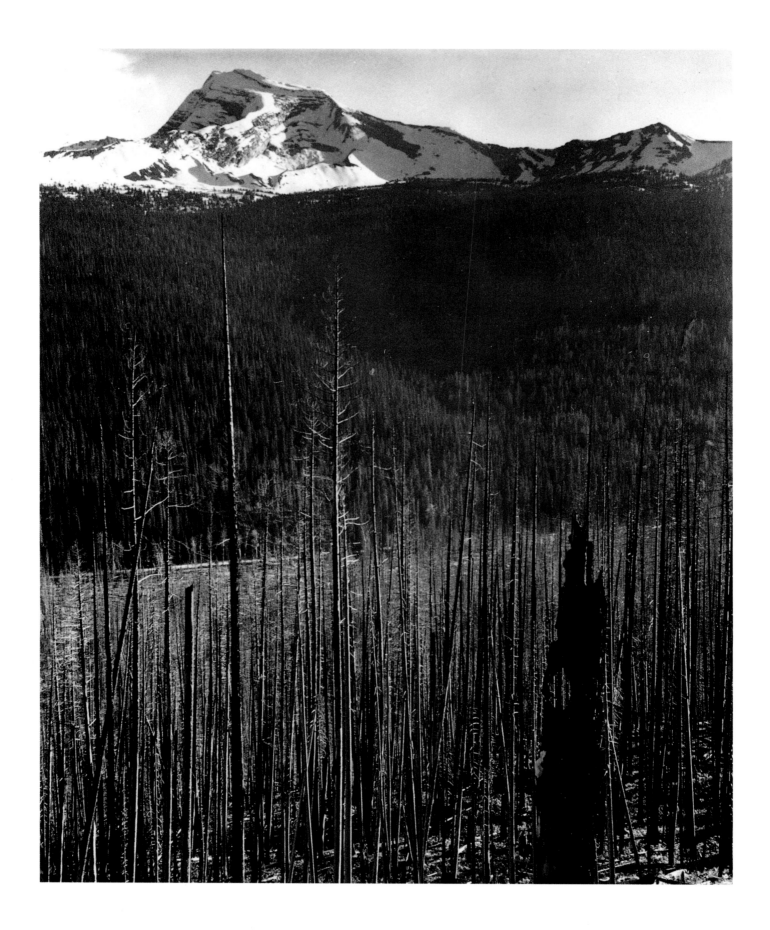

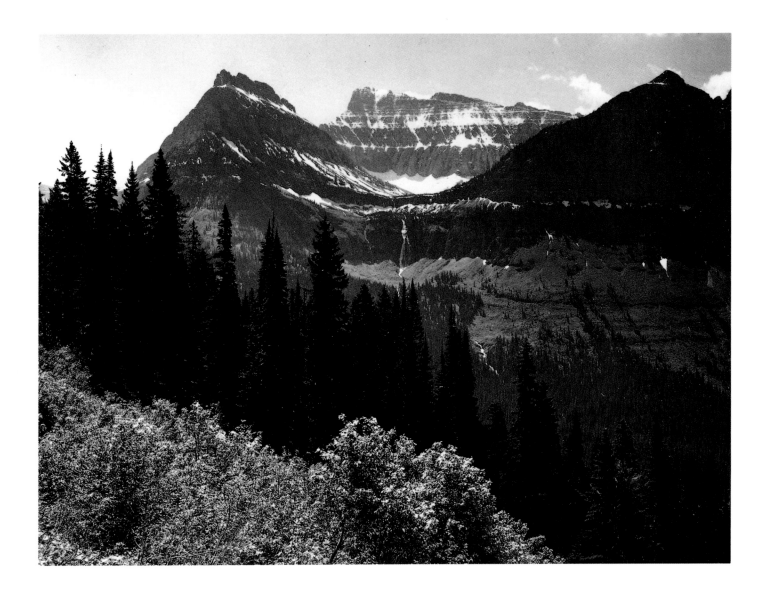

In Glacier National Park

The photographer's process of sorting an image into visually interesting zones of light blends flawlessly with the subject of the picture. The foreground is defined by light, leafy trees, set against a midground of dark pines and the more muted gray tones of the mountains in the far background. A dialogue is established between the highlights of the leaves in the foreground and the distant snow drifts.

Burned Area, Glacier National Park

This is one of the very few images in Adams' parks series in which nature is not in perfect harmony with itself. One is left to ponder the cause and consequences of the conflagration, and whether this was really the sort of thing the Interior Department had in mind when they commissioned Adams to do a series of murals. In any event, Ansel was never much concerned with following very strictly his employer's orders.

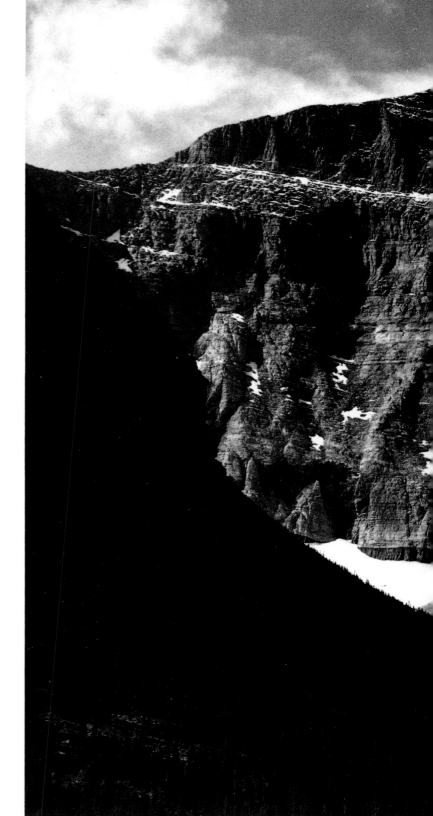

**From Going-to-the-Sun Chalet,
Glacier National Park**

A powerful, semicircular area of
shadow in the foreground and a
corresponding border of deep gray
sky frame this image of snowy
highlights against a richly toned
rock face. Horizontal lines of rock
strata play off against the vertical
weathering of the cliff side.

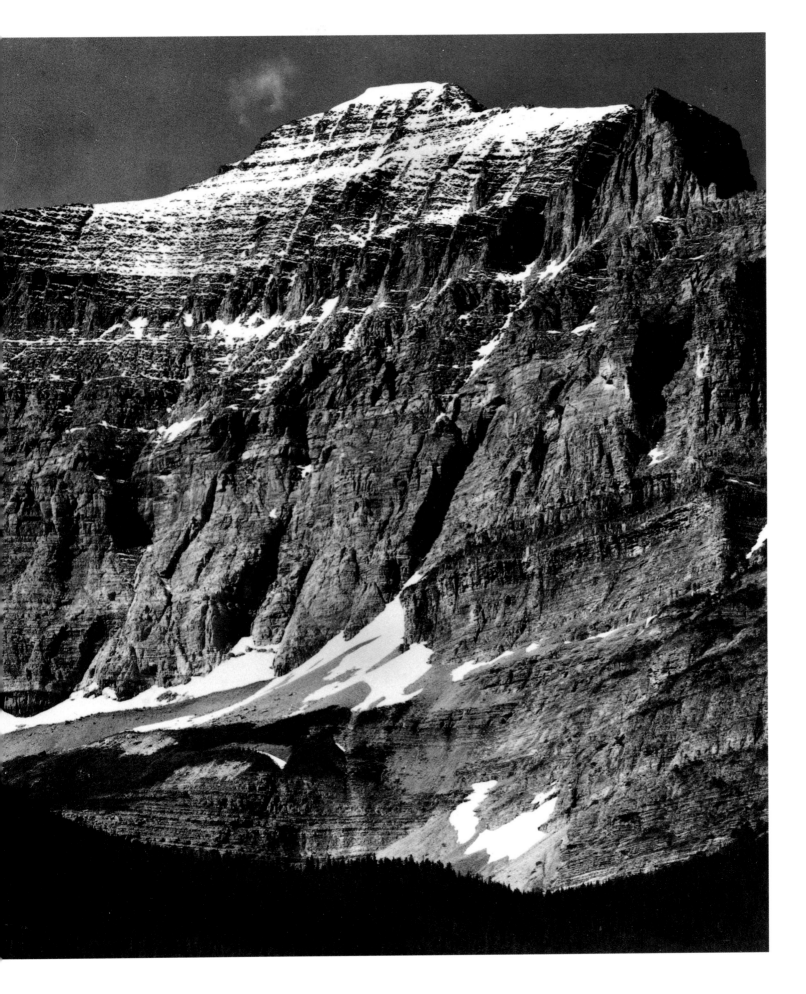

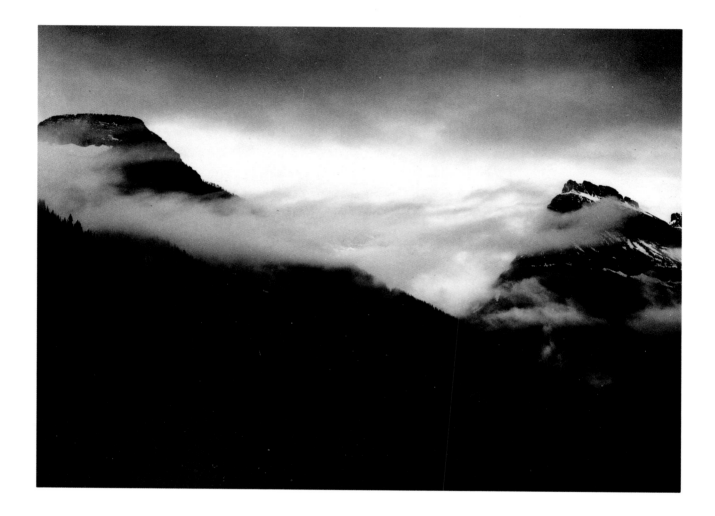

In Glacier National Park

This superb image is one of Ansel's moodier and more epic expressions, presaging the scale and impact of mature works such as *Winter Sunrise, Lone Pine*. Black tones are overwhelming here, both in the massive ridge that divides the picture diagonally and in the border of black sky. Low-lying clouds give the mountain faces a solemn, brooding quality.

From Logan Pass, Glacier National Park

A silvery, abstract swath of snow flows across the dark foreground of this
image. The smooth, broad forms in the foreground lead the eye to the intricate
detail of the border of pines in the midground and to the finely engraved
detail of the cliff face against brilliant highlights of snow in the background.

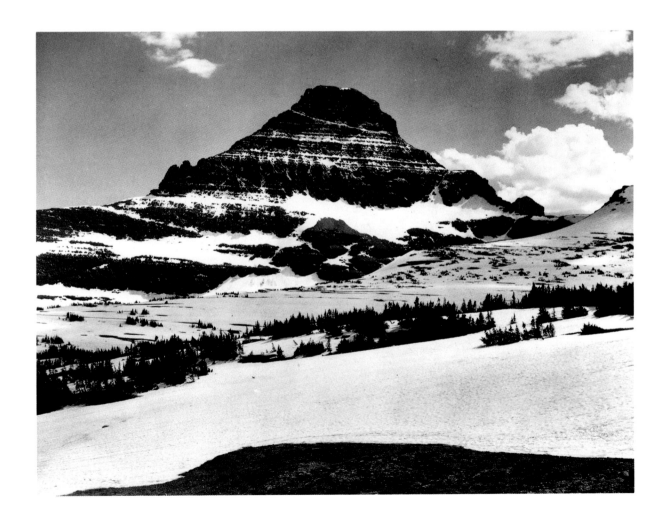

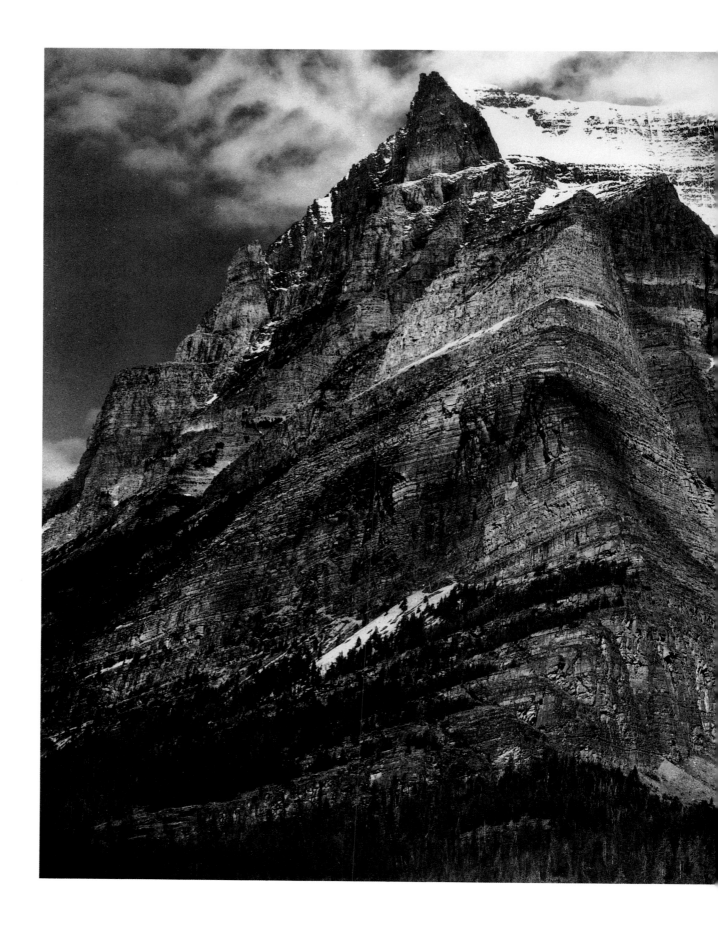

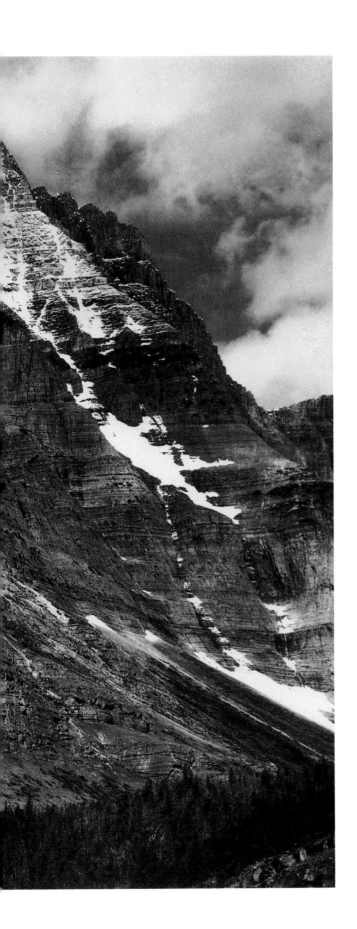

Going-to-the-Sun Mountain, Glacier National Park
The up-close framing of the mountain and the darkened
sky give this image a rhythmic, moody feel. The eye
scans upward from the dark base for the relief of lighter
tones, passing over the subtle gradations of the cliff face
in the midground to the pure white highlights of snow.

In Glacier National Park
This is a magisterial view of highlighted clouds floating
over a darkened valley and shadowed, snowy peaks.
Dark pines cut vertically against the muted grays of the
mountains in the background, leading the eye toward
the range of contrasts in a sky that fills half the image.

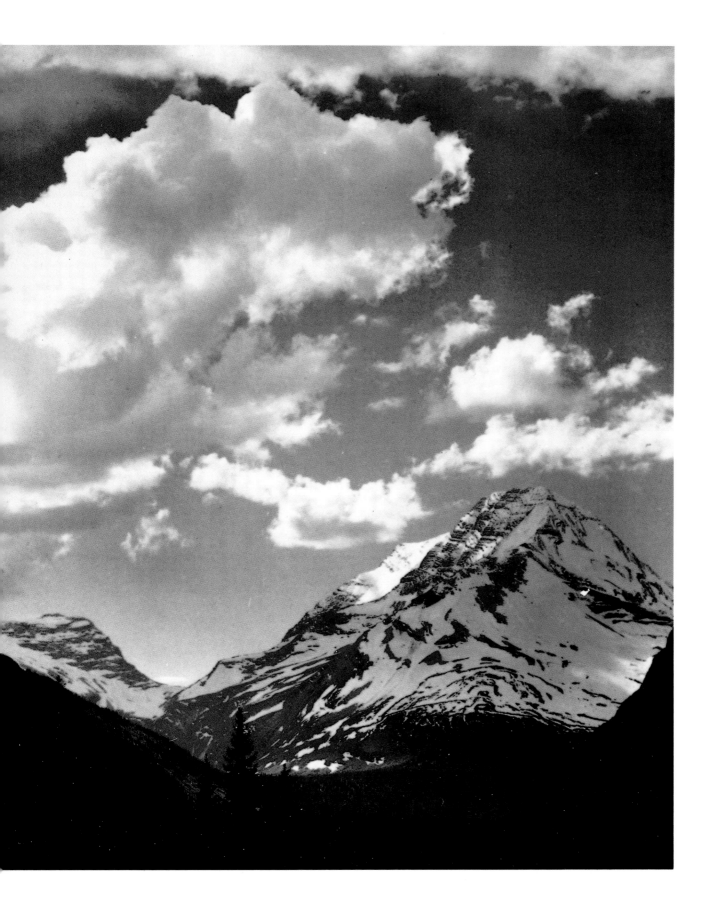

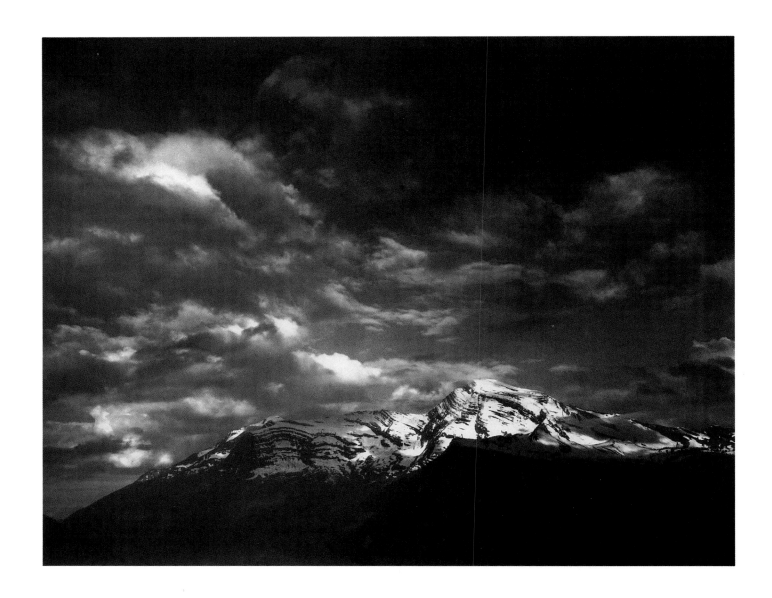

Heaven's Peak
This is a grandly operatic image of a brilliant snowcap set above
a deep black border of shadow. The top two-thirds of the image
is filled with tempestuous clouds, leading up to the deep black
of the open sky. The effect is to make the light on the mountaintop
appear to be in a heroic struggle against the darkness.

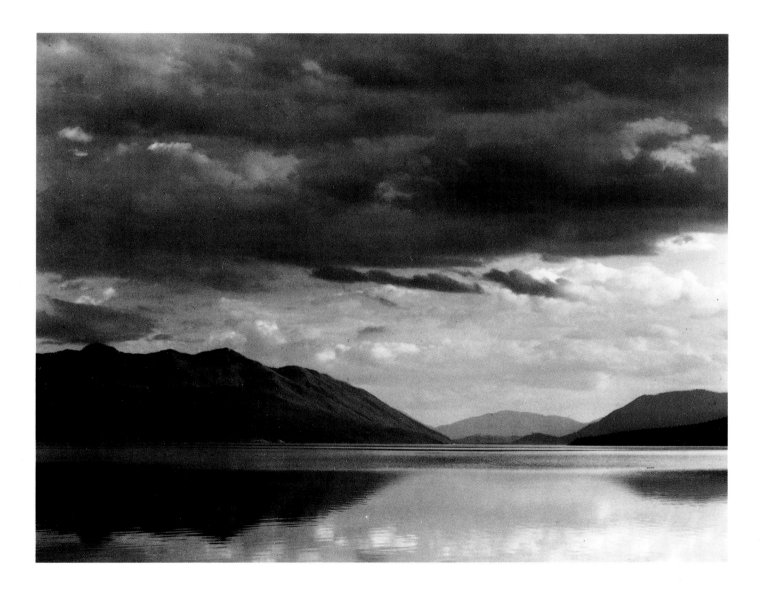

Evening, McDonald Lake, Glacier National Park
The dark bands of clouds that fill the upper half of this image serve to
dislocate the viewer's vantage point. Suddenly, clouds and mountains
seem to be of equal visual weight, floating on banks of lighter clouds
and silvery water. The reflection of the mountain in the lake surface
leads to further complex interrelations of forms throughout the image.

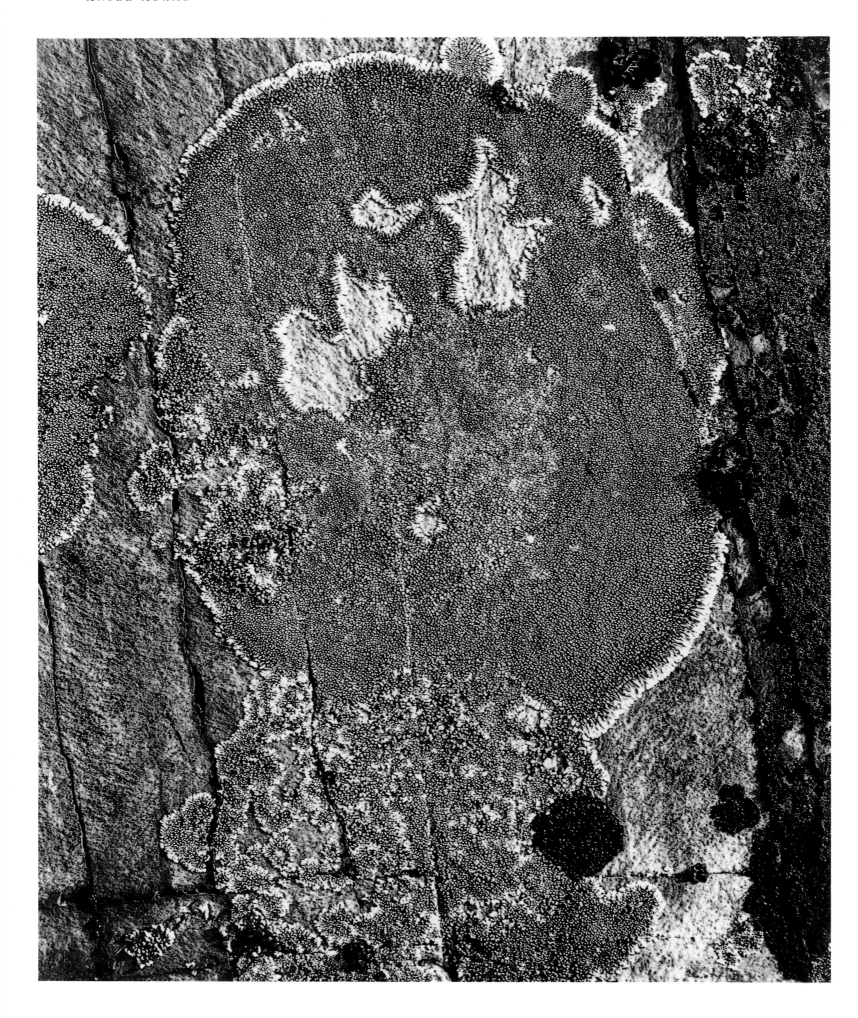

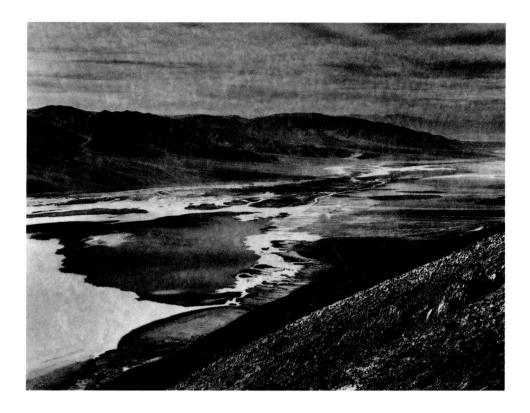

Death Valley National Monument

This plate is a virtuoso exercise in texture and tone. The eye is attracted first to the sharply engraved quality of the triangular area of rocks in the right foreground, and then past a black diagonal with some areas of detail to the dazzling white abstraction of the midground and the soft gray tones of the distant hills.

Lichen, Glacier National Park

This close-up view of a lichen growth plays with the viewer's sense of scale in the same way that the close-up of Jupiter Terrace does (see page 134). One is not sure at first exactly how large the object is—it could almost be an aerial shot on the scale of the corn field in page 49. Minute details of texture are brought out by the rich range of tones.

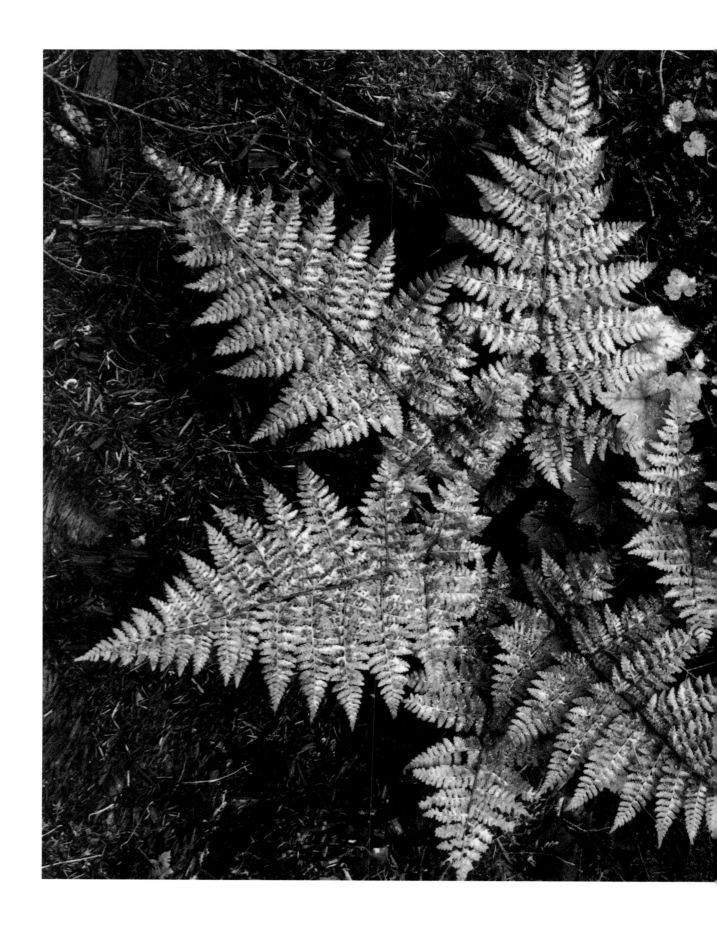

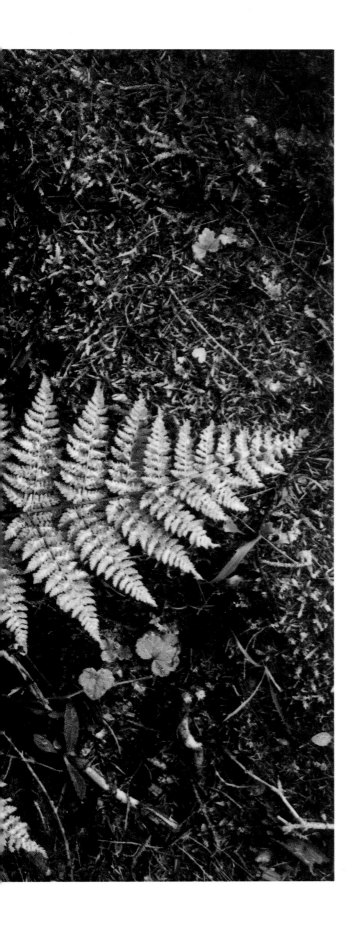

In Glacier National Park

Ansel captures the musical, rhythmic quality of organic forms in this close-up of a star-shaped fern. The eye follows the articulation of the branches outward from the center and then back toward the middle after recognizing that each smaller branch contains the structure of the plant in miniature. The effect is of a charmingly balanced rondo.

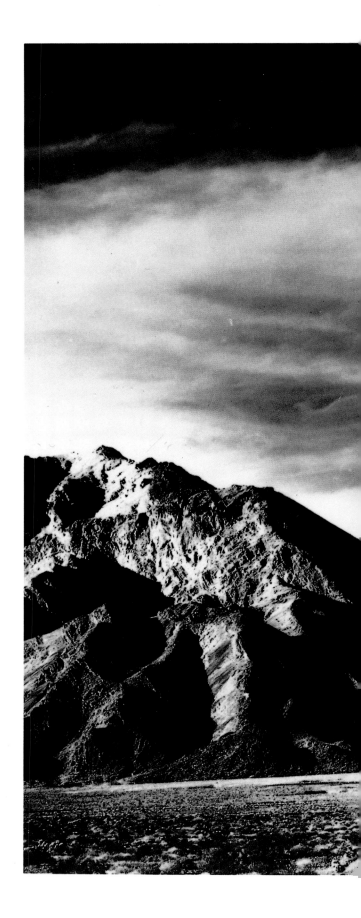

Near Death Valley

Deep pools of black shadow emphasize the inhuman
aspect of Death Valley, which was recently upgraded
by Congress from a national monument to the largest
national park within the contiguous states. In this
image, two diagonals challenge the eye: the strong
descent of the dark slope and the rise of light clouds.

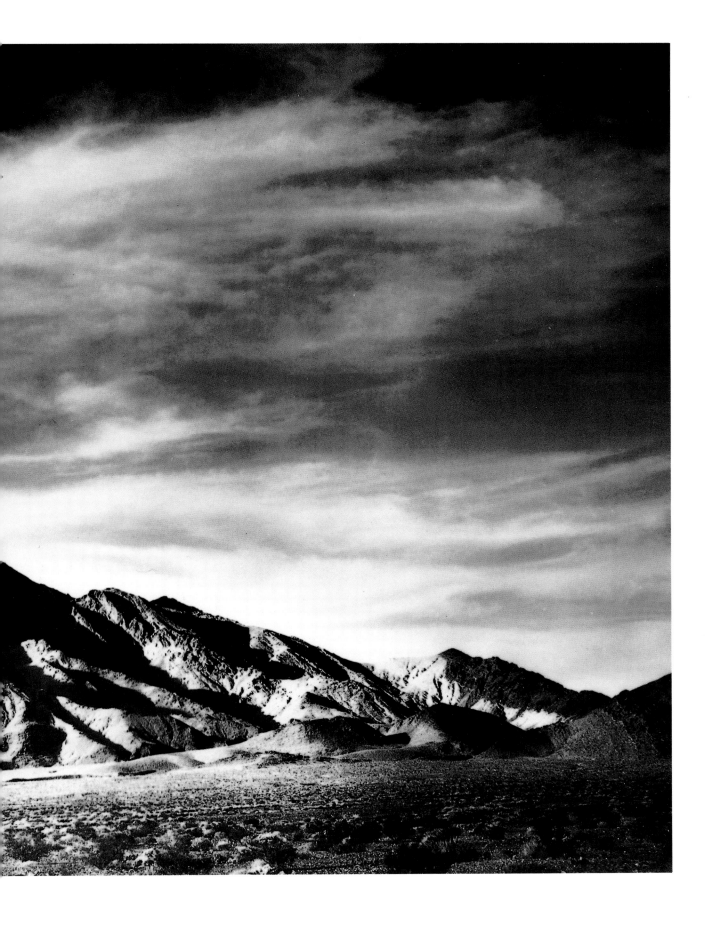

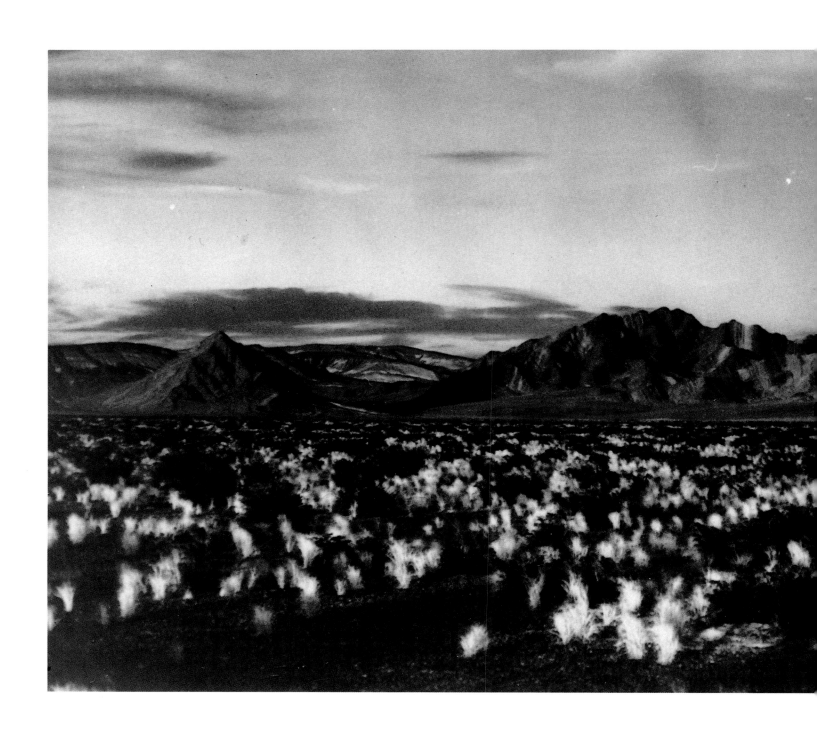

Near Death Valley National Monument

This plate shows how critical composition is in determining the emotional expression of a photograph. In comparison with the preceding photograph, the inclusion of light-colored vegetation in
the foreground makes the desert environment seem a less forbidding place. The windblown quality
of the vegetation is an interesting visual contrast with the permanence of the distant mountains.

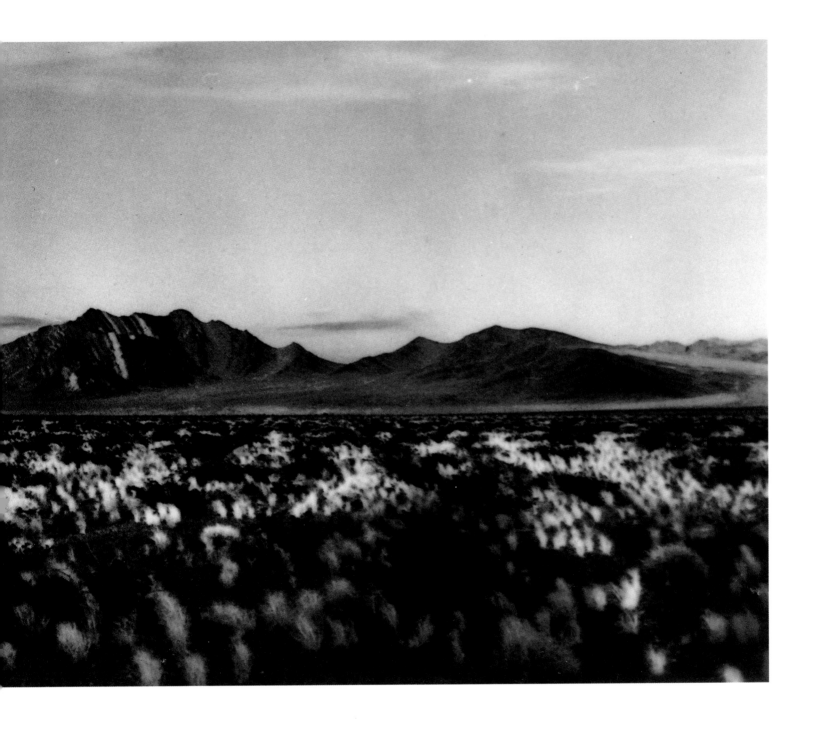

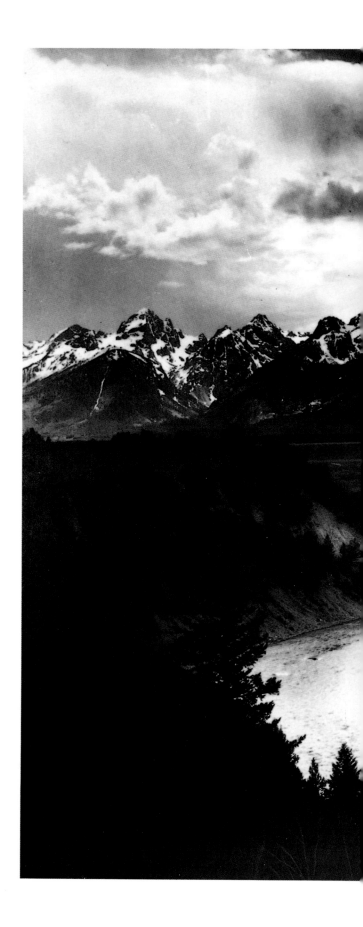

The Tetons—Snake River

The silvery highlight of the Snake River makes a
serpentine path through the center of this horizontal
composition as it passes richly varied tones of gray
and black. Because of a moderately long exposure,
the water expresses a sense of flow and motion,
while the mountains stand in sharply detailed relief.

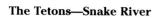

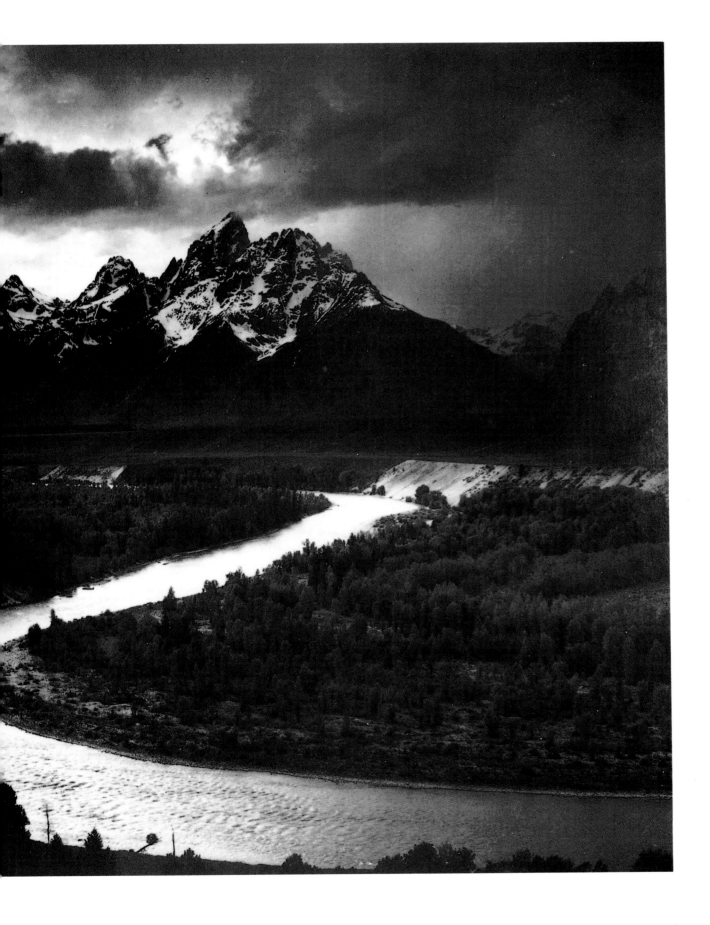

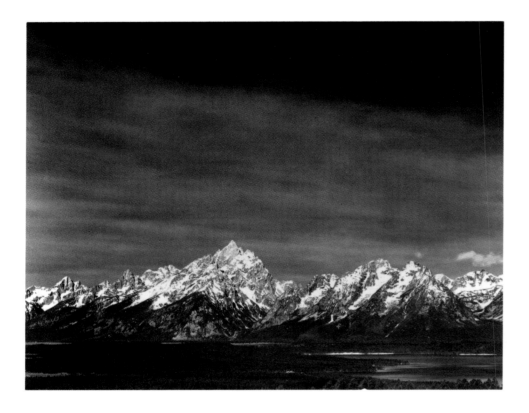

Tetons from Signal Mountain
The vast expanse of soft gray clouds, which takes up fully two-thirds of this
image, emphasizes the remote, regal quality of the mountains standing in isolation
from the low, darker foreground. The highlight of the bright snow on the peaks
leads the viewer across the complex edge of peaks through the center of the image.

Grand Teton
Here is an image reduced to its purest elements: a tall tree defined by
highlights and shadow, an expressive brushstroke of clouds against a
darkened sky, and a sharply defined mountainscape reflected in calm water.
The wispy cloud, the most ephemeral element of the picture, occupies
center stage, a beautiful passing moment in the still mountain setting.

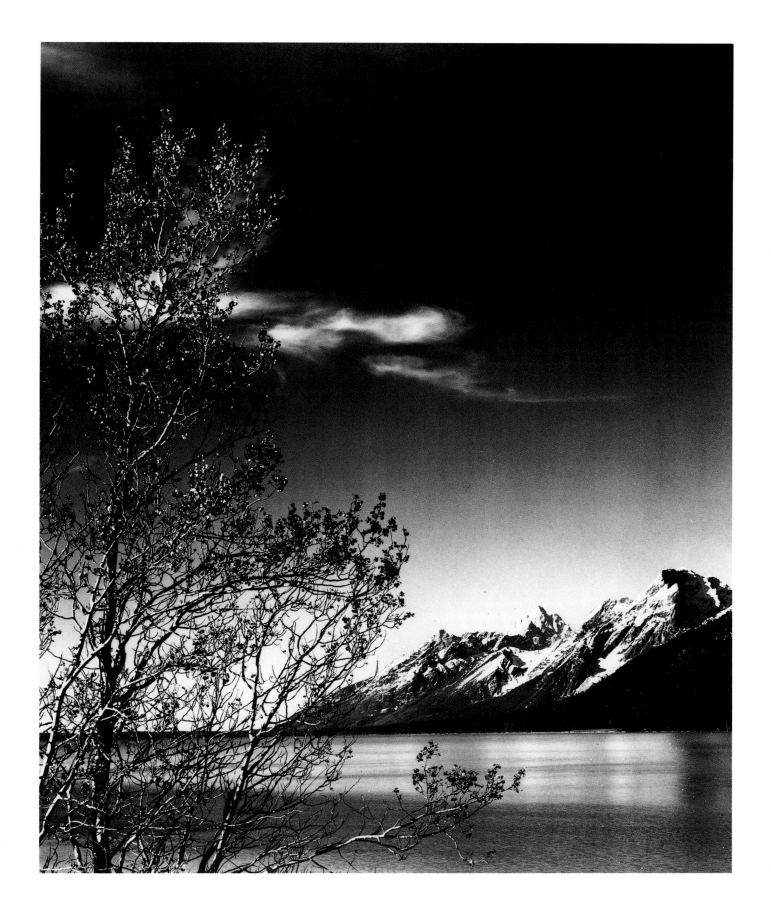

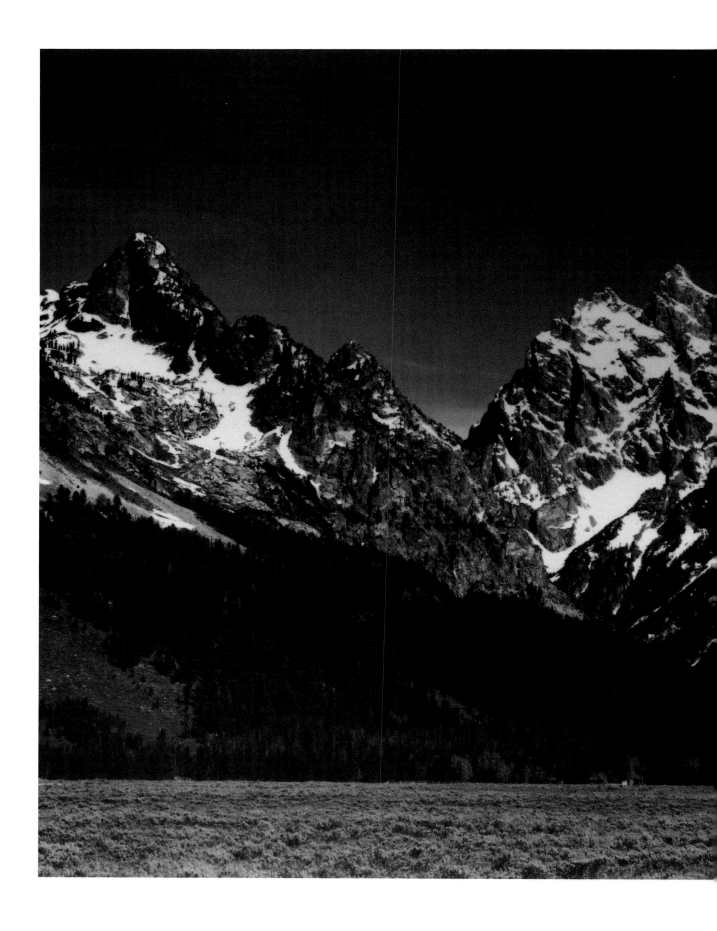

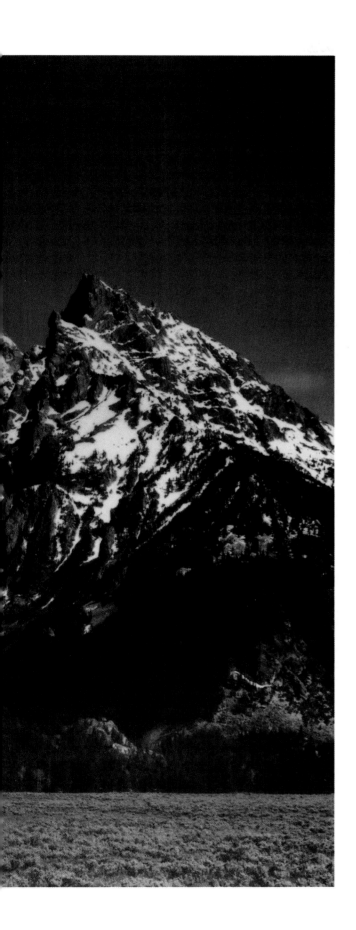

Grand Teton

This plate is a boldly composed horizontal image of mountains rising abruptly out of the plains. The gray border of vegetation in the foreground serves as both a frame and a point of reference for the sharp change in altitude. The level borderline of the foreground is a visual counterpoint to the jagged profile of the mountains. The eye reads the peaks almost like a line of music.

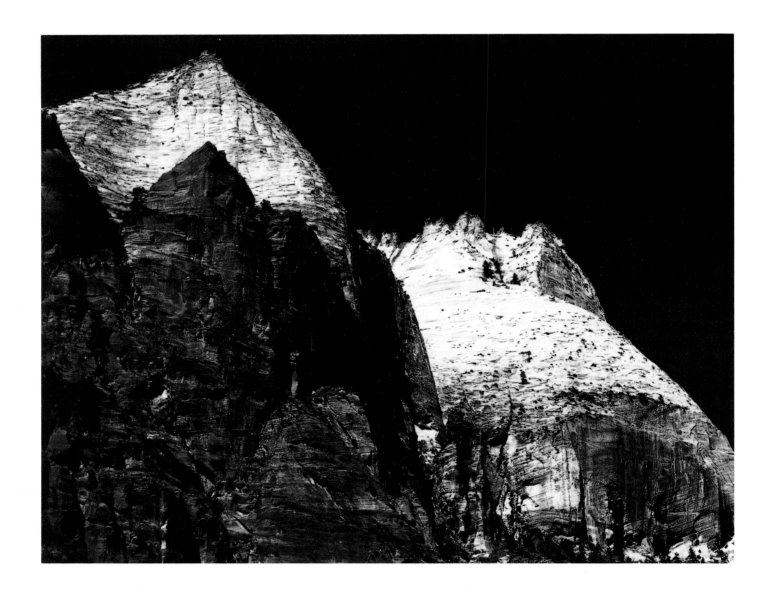

Zion National Park

Brilliantly defined white highlights stand out against a darkened sky in this superbly composed image from 1941. The effect is rather lunar, emphasizing the barren, inhospitable quality of the peaks. A zigzag form is echoed three times: by the edge of the dark sky against the white peaks, by the steplike band of white on the cliff face, and by the dark gray peaks in the foreground.

CHAPTER THREE

THE SPIRIT OF WILD PLACES

The Murals Project

In 1941, Secretary of the Interior Harold Ickes commissioned Ansel as a "Photo-Muralist" to photograph the widely varied national parks, national monuments, Indian lands, and reclamation projects administered by the department. Ickes was familiar with Adams' work after having purchased a mural screen with a blow-up of leaves and ferns executed by Ansel in 1936.

Several painters had been commissioned to provide murals for the new Interior Department building, but Adams was the first photographer. Ansel took on the huge project with customary enthusiasm. He had already had a good experience with the machinations of government offices when he presented a series of images of Kings River Canyon to Congress in 1936 in order to lobby for designating the region a national park. In 1940, just before Ansel started on the Murals Project, Kings River became a national park.

The project was to provide only a small number of photographic murals for the new Interior building, but Ansel felt deeply that the parks merited a thorough documentation. He took an extraordinary series of 225 photographs between October of 1941 and late June of 1942—not bad work for a photographer who considered a dozen images a year a good output! His photographic odyssey covered interior landscapes in eight western states—California, Arizona, New Mexico, Utah, Colorado, Wyoming, Montana, and Washington—for which he was paid the highest going rate at the time for outside consultants: $22.22 a day, plus expenses. The agreement was that Adams would contribute prints to the Interior Department but would retain control of the negatives in order to supervise the final printing.

This series of images, along with the Kings River Canyon photos, make up the plates in this book.

Unfortunately, the murals project was cut short by the entry of the United States into World War II. Ansel argued that his work was important in providing a record of "why we fight," but funding was cut off for the project in late June of 1942. Ansel would later resume his documentation of the national parks with two grants from the Guggenheim Foundation in 1946 and 1948. With these grants he produced the book *My Camera in the National Parks* and the portfolio *The National Parks and Monuments*. Adams' photographs remain an unprecedented chronicling of our national parks, both in breadth and in aesthetic value.

The Home Front

At the outset of World War II, Beaumont Newhall enlisted in the Army Air Corps and served in Italy. More of the work at the Museum of Modern Art fell to Nancy Newhall and to Adams himself, as vice president of the photography committee. Ansel's work for the Museum of Modern Art brought the outdoorsman more into the orbit of New York City for several weeks a year. His feelings about the city were, at best, mixed. He enjoyed the energetic pace of the city, the occasional days of good weather in the spring, and the friendship of artists such as Charles Sheeler, but on overcast days the museum began to look more like a mausoleum to him.

"My inner vision sought the Sierra and the Pacific shores," he wrote in his autobiography, and he asked himself, "What in hell am I doing here, far from home and family and Yosemite?"

Ansel's state of mind may be read into his mysterious image titled *MoMA Sculpture Garden, New York*

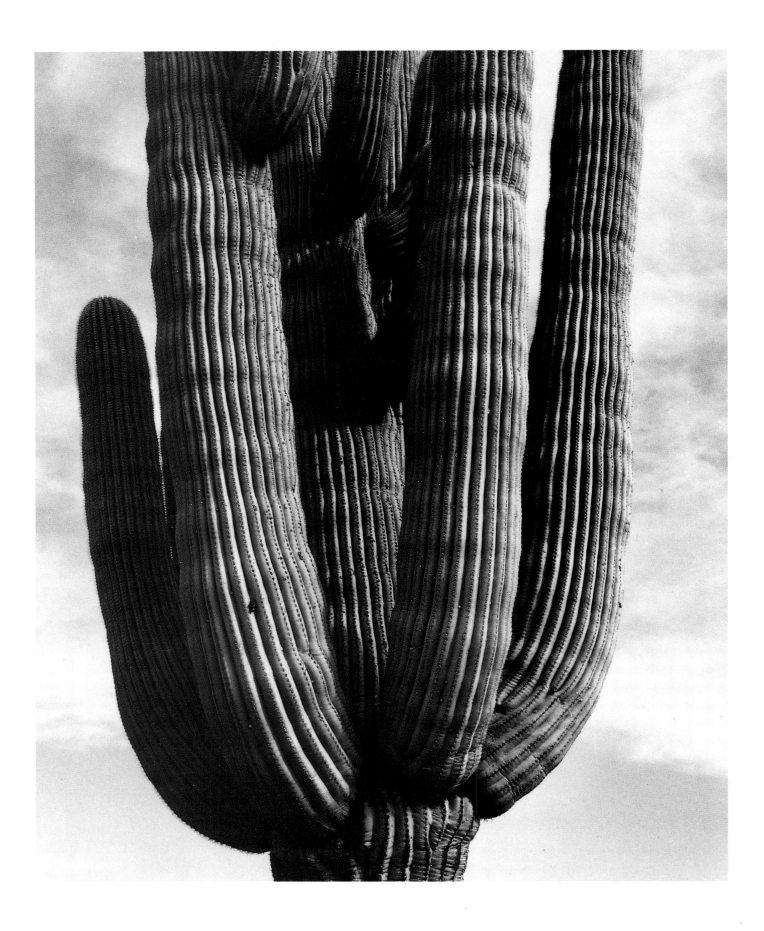

City (c. 1945). The leafless, somewhat blighted-looking young trees stand out starkly against the misty background of the sculpture garden, which dissolves into a ghostly, almost intangible skyline. The sculpture itself has a middle value between the black lines of trees and the insubstantial buildings. The trees, planted in circles of bricks, look regimented, like prisoners, yet they are the most vital thing in the yard. They looked trapped by the products made by man, but seem more likely to endure because of their rich black contrast.

The light in the photo overall is not the clear, celestial light of the Sierras but a dissipated city light that seems to bleed out the scene. A sculpture in the shape of a giant lollipop in sharp focus in the foreground echoes the tree trunks in their brick bases, but it looks lopsided and askew. The artwork is not an adequate substitute for nature, which may have been what Ansel was experiencing at the time. In the middle ground on the left, a photographer with a tripod frames a piece of sculpture. The photographer in the scene seems almost incidental, like clutter pushed off to the side, rather than the heroic image of a photographer in Yosemite as a rapt observer of nature.

Though an avowed pacifist, Ansel longed to make himself useful to the war effort. The army was not much interested in a forty-year-old man with young dependents, so Ansel volunteered as a civilian to show troops around Yosemite Valley and helped print classified negatives of the Japanese bases in the Aleutians. Adams' major wartime project, however, was documenting the lives of the 110,000 Japanese-American citizens who were interned at

Saguaro

In this close-up view of a giant cactus, the tones range from full black to bright white in undulating bands. The cropped composition, which shows neither the base nor the top of the cactus, leads the eye upward along the bands of light and shadow so that the viewer's appreciation of the light becomes identical with the organic structure of the saguaro.

Saguaros, Saguaro National Monument

The unusual shapes of the giant cactuses in Saguaro National Monument are presented as an orchestration of medium gray tones. Unlike many of Adams' images, there are no large zones of deep black or bright white. The subtle variations of gray bring out the pleated structure of the saguaros.

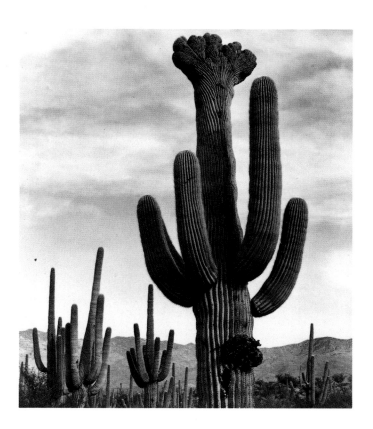

the Manzanar War Relocation Camp in the Owens Valley in the High Sierra of California.

In an unprecedented move in the United States, thousands of American citizens of Japanese descent were deprived of their civil rights under the constitution, rounded up, and interred during the war years at Manzanar under President Roosevelt's Executive Order 9066. Ansel, in perhaps a misguided propaganda attempt, desired to show the courage and dignity of these people. Some of his best friends had mixed feelings about the result, published in the book *Born Free and Equal*. Dorothea Lange said: "It

99

was shameful. That's Ansel. . . . He's ignorant in these matters. He isn't acutely aware of social change. It was far for him to go. He felt pretty proud of himself for being such a liberal."

The book itself is a rather idealized, unidimensional view of camp life. The cover image, *Young Man, Manzanar Relocation Center, California* (1943), has the sentimental simplicity of a Chinese communist propaganda poster, with a resolutely noble-looking man surveying the sunlit valley. The man himself is a cipher, as monumental as a tree stump, revealing no particular interiority. Perhaps Ansel did not fully comprehend how a figure in a landscape becomes the central focus and mediates the viewer's emotional response. In *Young Man*, the valley is timeless but the stolidity of the subject is not fully transcended.

Still Life, Yonemitsu Family Quarters, Manzanar Relocation Center, California (1943) is positively mawkish as subject matter; a framed picture of a young Japanese man in an American military uniform, signed "Bob," stands against a picture of an Asian-looking Christ, next to a small gourd and a hand-tied paper bow. The photo communicates in the way that a sign does, dictating its content: good American boy, patriot, writes his family, believes in God, eats exotic vegetables, and has a few native handicrafts but on the whole is just like us.

The portrait *A Young Lawyer and His Family, Manzanar Relocation Center, California* (1943) shows a young couple with their young son making do in a poor yet clean environment, reinforcing the overlaid view of general humility, cheerfulness, and industriousness that Adams meant to convey. Ansel later wrote that his goal with the book was simply to document how the people at Manzanar rose above their conditions. Dorothea Lange and other photographers for the War Relocation Authority came much closer to the psychological reality of the internees. Their images are of families wearing identification tags like furniture, a bewildered child knee-high to a soldier's leg, and the desolate banality of the stalaglike camp.

Images of a Cosmic Mind

Despite his drawbacks as a social historian, Adams produced two of his most spectacularly visionary images, *Mount Williamson, Sierra Nevada, From Manzanar, California* (1944) and *Winter Sunrise, Sierra Nevada, from Lone Pine, California* (1944), during this period at Manzanar. He may not have had any particular insight into the psychology of the detainees at the relocation camp, but he was always finely attuned to the subtleties of the natural environment.

The Owens Valley where Manzanar was situated was near his beloved Sierra Range, which rose dramatically more than 11,000 feet straight up from the desert floor. Ansel took Mount Williamson from the rooftop platform of his car, parked amid a field of boulders stretching several miles back to the base of Mount Williamson. He felt that the vagaries of light in the desert, and the difficulty of composing the foreground and distant peaks as the mind's eye perceived them, made the conditions unsuitable for color photography and generally a disappointment in black and white. However, the photographer set up his 8-by-10 view camera just as a dramatic storm was passing through the mountains. The afternoon sun shone through the clouds, creating intense shadows and strong contrast with the bright clouds near the sun. Everything from the boulders in the foreground to the distant peaks was in sharp focus.

The result is nothing less than a Edenic view of God's relationship with nature. For Ansel, the world is alive with light. The beams of light appear like a benediction from a glowing, limitless higher realm. Light is the unifying element, taking the eye from the rough facets of the boulders in the foreground to the

In Zion National Park
This plate is a dramatic composition of deep blacks, brilliant highlights, and richly varied tones of gray. The angle from below leads the eye toward the well-defined forms and clean edges of the rock surface.

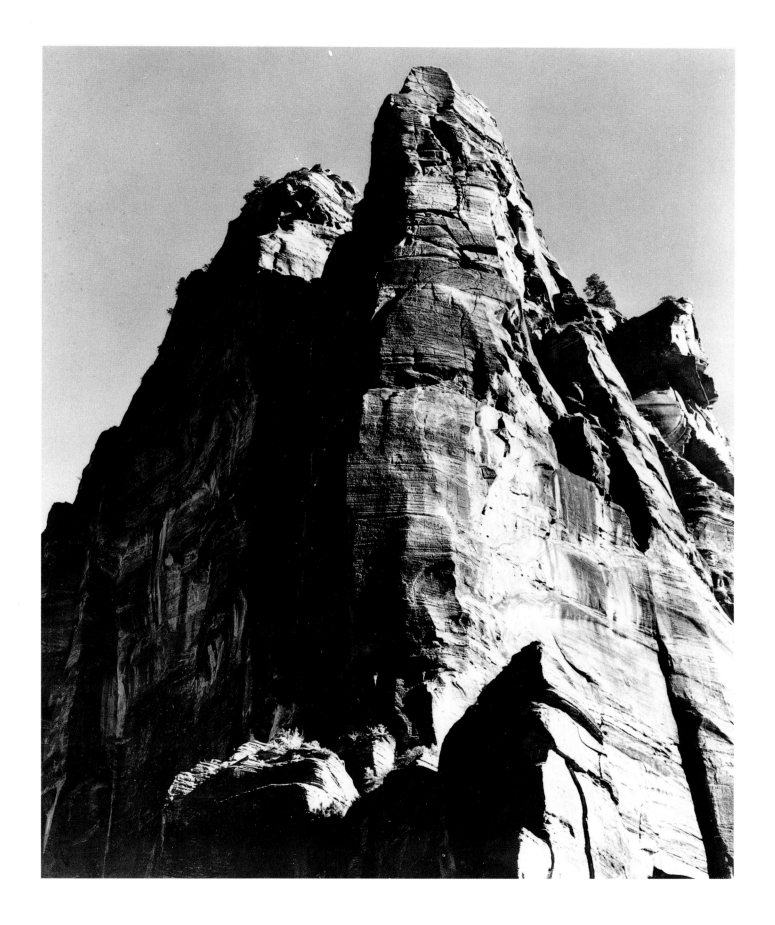

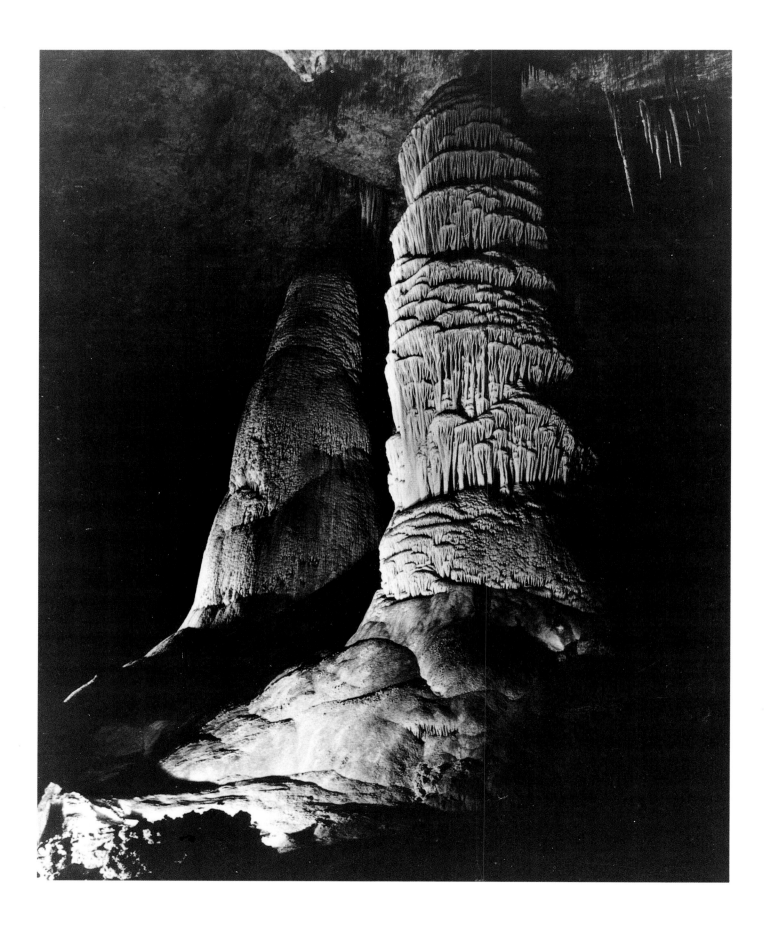

midground on which the shafts of light fall like a spotlight, up to the distant peaks and the low-lying, brilliant clouds. Finally, the light beams take us up and out of the frame and this plane of existence. The transition is incredible, from the rocky materialness of the boulders to the immaterial and ineffable realm of light, yet the movement is seamless, leading from pure stone to pure light, with no break in gradation.

All is one in Ansel's spiritual view. A momentary passage of light takes on the weight and significance of stone. At the same time, the boulders themselves seem somehow fragile and transitory, creatures of light poised on a balance of light and dark. Without the life-giving power of light, all is void and formless. It is just this sense of the continuity of permanence and impermanence that draws us again and again to Adams' images. His photos are deep, not only in the composition from near to far, but in the unity of form and subject.

Winter Sunrise, Sierra Nevada, from Lone Pine, California (1944), made during the same period, is so perfect that it doesn't appear to be produced by human hands. To begin with, it is a marvelously modern composition, with a dazzlingly bold swath of black shadow running fluidly like spilled ink across the midground, the etched crystalline detail of the snowcaps, the deep gray of the sky, and the tenderly illuminated highlights of the trees in the foreground. The print resembles the pure, clean edges of a negative itself.

Then there is that perfect, unbelievable detail of a black horse grazing placidly on a spotlit patch of

The Giant Dome. Largest stalagmite thus far discovered. It is sixteen feet in diameter and estimated to be sixty million years old. Hall of Giants, Big Room. Ansel's photo of the underground caves in Carlsbad Caverns National Park, New Mexico, is something of a qualified success. Artificial lighting gives a theatrical sense to the rocks rather than a truly felt expression of wonder. Even the unusually wordy title is evidence of trying too hard.

ground. Surely, this can only have been stage managed in heaven. The detail of the horse makes the scale of the picture shift dizzily to a sweeping mountain vista, captured in an impossible moment of balance when all the accidental details of a natural scene seemed to have combined to form a classical composition. The picture has the charm and effortless feel of a snapshot, yet at the same time the sense of something eternal.

The eye and mind volley back and forth between these two perceptions. You cannot stay in one mode for too long without merging imperceptibly into the other point of view—classical versus momentary, purely abstract versus purely naturalistic, monumental versus intimate. Ultimately, like all of Adams' best work, the picture is a unity. Opposing elements shade into one another until they are one. This image is one of Ansel's most powerfully felt statements about his worldview: that everything in nature has a place, and everything has value if it can be understood in relation to the whole.

Adams recalled a bit of scrambling straight out of a silent comedy that went into the making of this picture. He waited, shivering in near-zero temperature, for the sunlight to hit a certain spot among the trees as a horse grazed with its backside turned to the photographer. Ansel clicked off a few exposures but the horse seemed resolutely indifferent to having its portrait taken. Just as the scene filled with sunlight, the horse turned obligingly in profile and Adams exposed the film. Moments later, the dramatic lighting conditions of strong sunlight and stark shadow were gone forever.

Typically, Ansel didn't spend much time explaining what should be felt by the viewer when looking at the image. Instead, he looked to the present-day devastation of the fragile desert ecology by the forces of urbanization in Southern California, particularly the wasteful consumption of water for homes and pools in Los Angeles. For the artist, *Winter Sunrise* was an enduring image of the way the land used to be, and could be again if people establish once more a reverence for the earth.

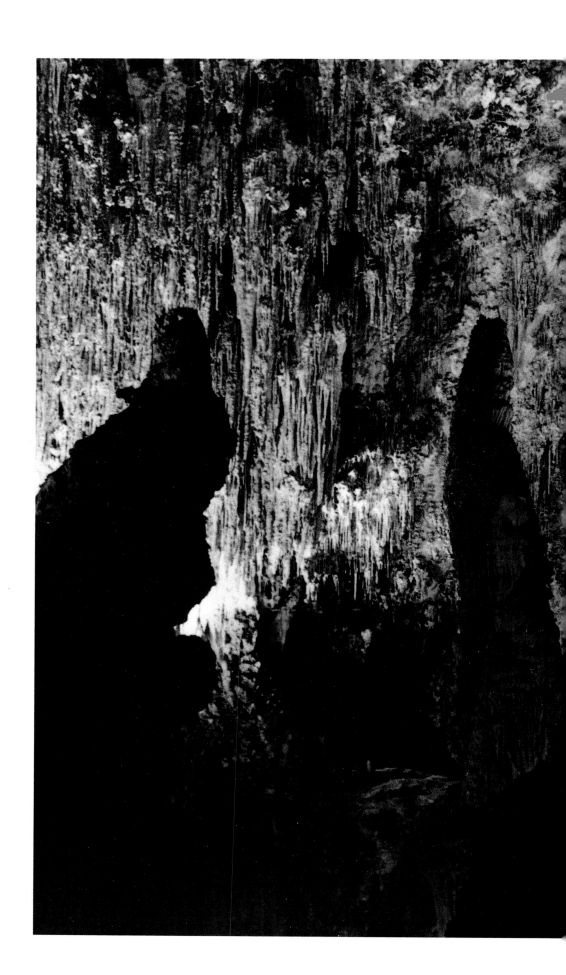

In the Queen's Chamber
This cavern could almost be a
set for Wagner's *Das Rheingold*,
so operatic is the sensibility
of its scale and lighting. There
are deep blacks, brilliant whites,
and rich tonalities, but the
unnatural light source prevents
this from being among Ansel's
greatest images, wherein he
seems to be participating in
an act of creation with nature.

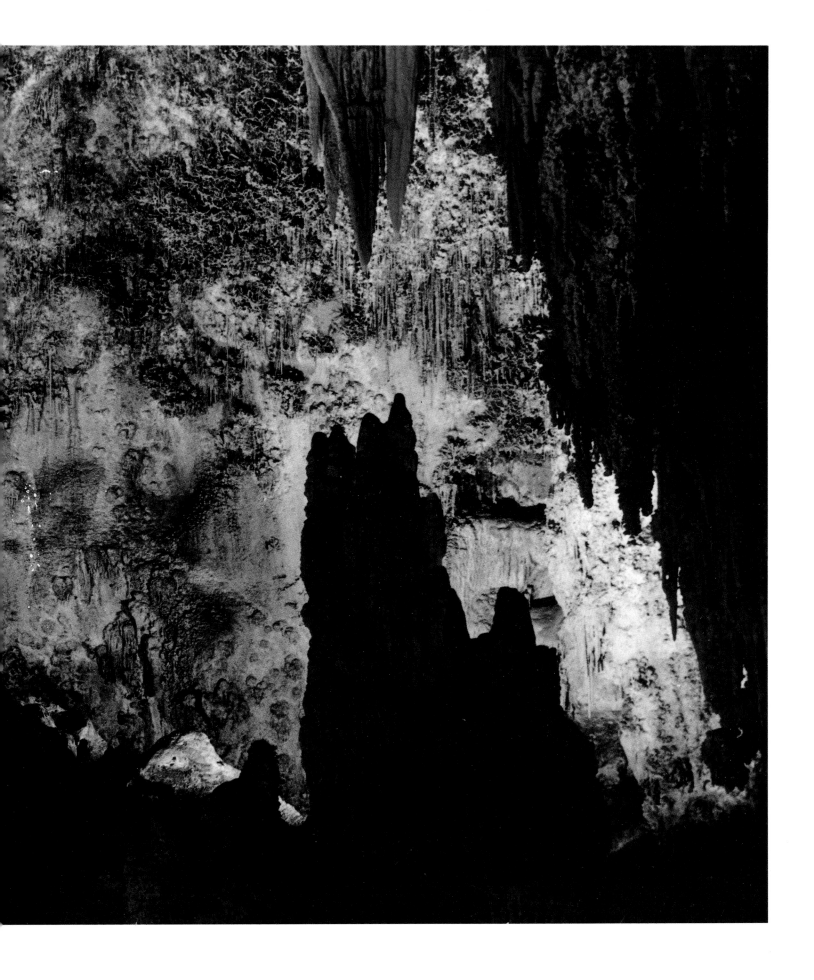

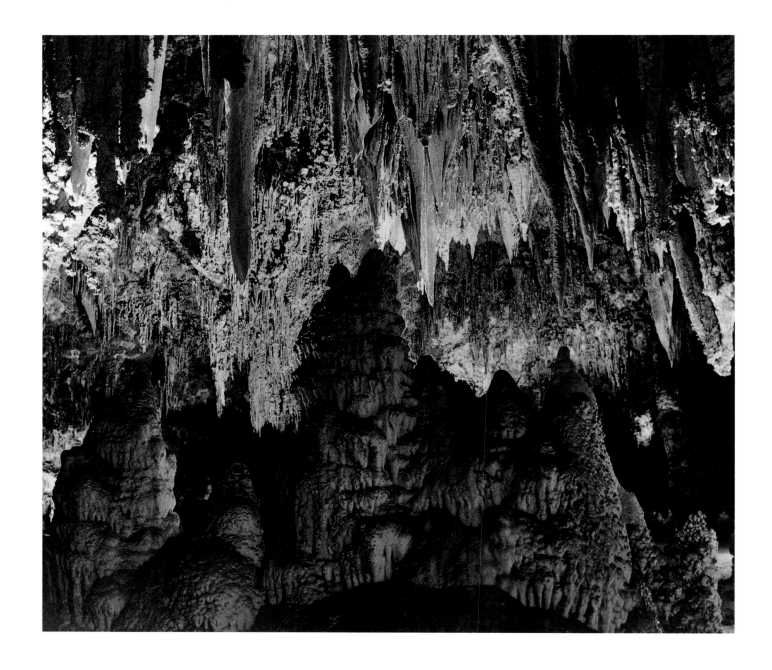

Formations along the wall of the Big Room, near Crystal Spring Dome

In many ways, these underground images presage the epic sense of
Adams' mature images. However, the forced quality of the melodramatic
lighting does not match his clean aesthetic sense, which did not seek
forced effects. The pictures, though visually intriguing, lack deep feeling.

The Philosophy of Photography

After the war, a split developed in the field of photography that would become as serious as the break between pictorialism and straight photography. The schism had been in the making for a long time, at least since the years of the Depression, when photographers began to winnow themselves out into two opposing camps. The camps may be defined as the social realists versus the more self-consciously arty photographers, but the split speaks more deeply to a question that still engages photographers—that is, photography which is mainly concerned with its subject versus photography used for expressive means.

Critics have weighed all sides, from the view that all photography is of necessity subject photography, to a denial that subject photography should even be considered expressive, and thence to the view that the distinctions are artificial to begin with and that it is all a continuity. Postmodernists love to flirt with the ambiguities of the subject versus expression; see, for instance, the work of Cindy Sherman, who makes the artificiality of her poses the content of the photograph.

The battle lines were clearly drawn by the late 1940s. On one side, at least conceptually, were the great social documentarians of the Depression: Walker Evans, Dorothea Lange, Berenice Abbott, and Margaret Bourke-White. Their leader was Edward Steichen, enormously successful as a commercial photographer and politically prominent in the art world. In the other camp were the group of modernists who had turned their back on the political turmoil of the Depression to pursue their personal visions—photographers like Edward Weston, Minor White, and, of course, Ansel Adams. Their aging and ailing standard-bearer was Alfred Stieglitz.

Methodology and intent separated the two schools as much as the nettlesome issue of content. Stieglitz's followers, among whom Adams fervently counted himself, belonged to an older photographic tradition. Most learned to photograph with view cameras, slow lenses, and slower film. Most preferred the quality of natural outdoor light, perhaps

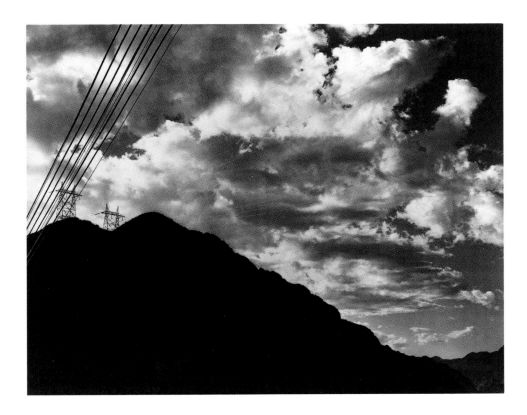

Boulder Dam

This plate exemplifies the Promethean qualities that the modernists attributed to technology. The image (from 1941) is as grandiose as any mural in Rockefeller Center. The cables at left seem to reach straight up into heaven to bring down the power of electricity to man. The brilliant clouds against the black hillside fairly sing the praises of a brighter tomorrow through electricity!

because the first generations of indoor lighting technology were so unreliable. They shared an almost reverential attitude toward exposing a negative; Ansel would go up in the High Sierra with only six fragile glass negatives per trip. Similarly, when Stieglitz was lugging his heavy camera rig through the Alps, he only exposed a plate when he knew all conditions were right. He lamented the "random firing" technique of the latter-day school.

Ansel was appalled when Margaret Bourke-White told him how she went about making an exposure. The creator of countless memorable images for *Life* magazine, such as the well-known portrait of Gandhi by his spinning wheel, would simply set her shutter at 1/100 of a second and click away at every lens stop from the most open down to f/22, with the confidence that one of them had to be correct.

Philosophy intermingles with technology and technique at this point. The older photographers, dating back to Timothy H. O'Sullivan and beyond, are celebrated for the intense, rapturous quality of their gaze. It could be argued that this clarity of vision stems from looking more deeply and shooting less often. On the other hand, something is lost by such a severe focus, and that is the spontaneous quality of human interaction. Ansel's portrait of a mischievous Georgia O'Keeffe, or that of Stieglitz's rare smile, show that he could shoot from the hip with the best of them, but these are departures from the current of his work rather than the mainstream.

The newer photographers, such as Garry Winogrand, may have sacrificed some image quality to capture their subjects, but at the same time gained a sense of life and immediacy in their work.

Boulder Dam Power Unit

This dynamically composed image is as much a tribute to the machine aesthetic as is a photo by Charles Sheeler or any of Adams' modernist counterparts. Ansel always was an iconoclastic mix of conservationist and pragmatist. He was in favor of the large government energy projects, and in his last days was an advocate of nuclear energy.

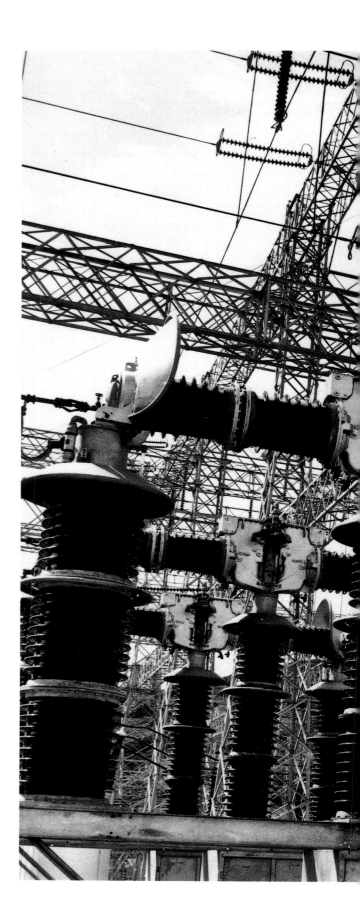

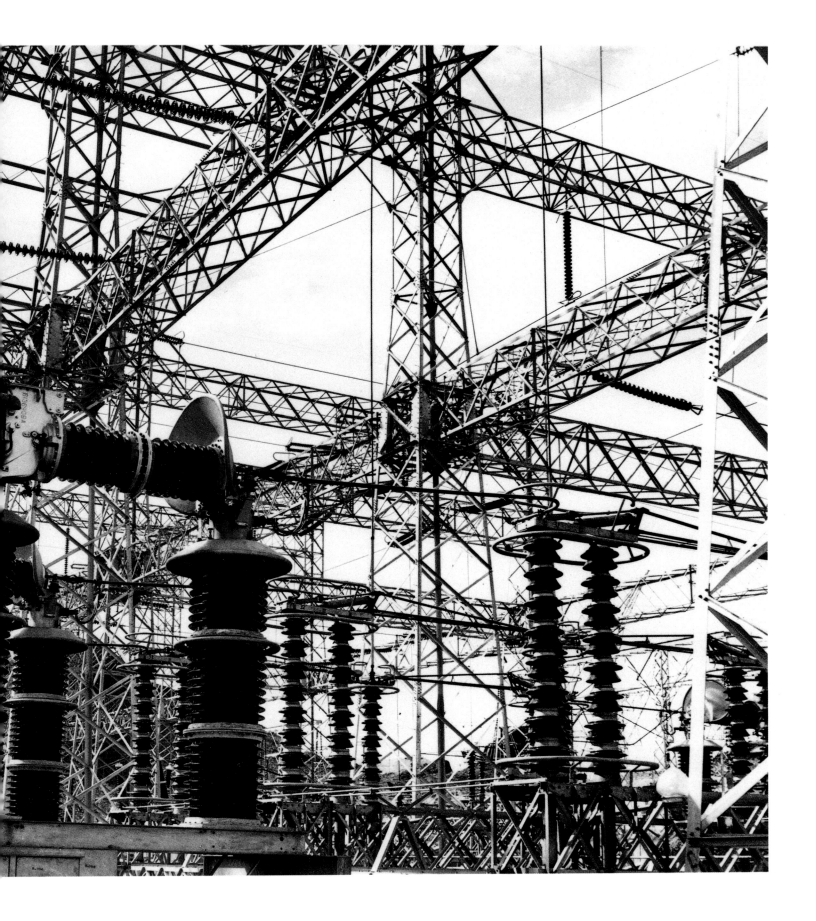

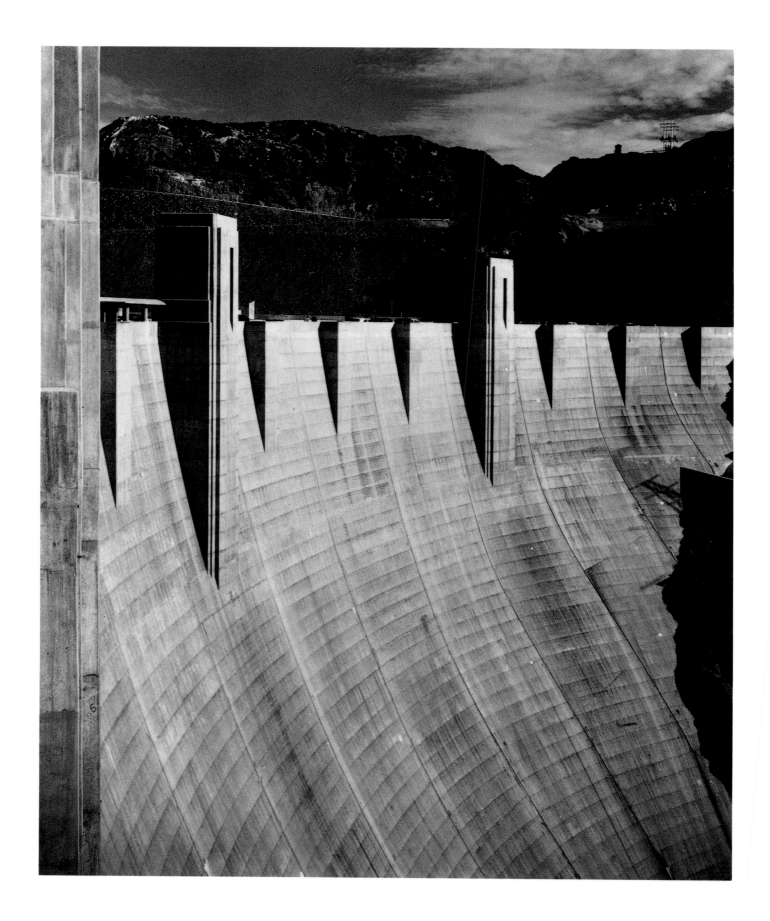

Subject and Style

All of the above points raise once again the issue of subject versus style. Photographs have an inherent interest because by and large they are about something. Nobody can deny that a hand-held flash picture of Jack Ruby shooting Lee Harvey Oswald is a compelling photograph, no matter what the technical drawbacks. America, convulsively violent nation that it is, even has a history of such assassination photos, dating back at least to William Warnecke's 1910 portrait of a blood-spattered Mayor William J. Gaynor in New York City. The horrified gaze of the mayor's aide and the stricken look of the mayor, appearing like a felled horse, still leap out of the frame despite the years. These are prime examples of subject photography—photographs that are chiefly interesting because of what they show rather than how they are done.

Ansel was interested in photographs at the other end of the continuum: photographs that expressed something personal about what the photographer felt. Perhaps polemically, Ansel lumped almost all of the social realists into the school of subject photography. Adams thought that Willard Van Dyke, a founding member of the Group f/64 movement, was particularly good at documenting images of social significance, but as a result Ansel came to view him as a kind of sociologist rather than an expressive photographer.

Adams dismissed the work of photographers for the Federal Public Works of Art Project as a hodgepodge of pictures of destitutes, May Day ceremonies, and oppressed workers. Walker Evans was singled out for special scorn. Ansel believed that

Boulder Dam

Ansel couldn't find much use for cities but he could enthusiastically support a project like a dam, which made life better for people and apparently did not harm the environment. The sheer surface of concrete in this image from 1942 appears like a natural formation; in fact it determines the horizon line for the peaks in the background.

Weston's images of seashells would endure long after Evans' portrait of "derelicts in a dingy doorway" was forgotten. In fact, both images have remarkable staying power, but for different reasons.

Ansel exempted only Dorothea Lange's images as having any true emotional resonance. He praised her photograph *White Angel Breadline* (1933) in particular as moving into a dimension beyond the subject. Indeed, the picture works strongly both as a document of the poverty during the Depression and as a more formally composed image. A man with a broken-crowned hat turns toward the viewer with his back to a crowd of faceless, better-dressed men. The eyes follow the shapes of the hats down to the man's empty tin cup and encircling arms with resolutely clasped hands. It is a haunting picture of a man beaten down in the struggle for survival, and at the same time an evocative synecdoche of the greater social background of the Depression.

Adams warned Lange about the totalitarian purposes to which documentary photography can be distorted. In particular, he resented the notion that photography was not important unless it was about a political subject. Rightly or wrongly, he railed that his close-ups of nature could have social significance equal to that of endless pictures of breadlines. He charged that Steichen in particular was afraid of confronting absolute beauty in an image. The reverse of course might also be said—that Adams was unwilling to look at the legitimate social role that photography can play.

At the other end of the spectrum, Berenice Abbott insists contentiously in the documentary film, *Berenice Abbott: A View of the 20th Century*, that "I think all photography is documentary, or it isn't even photography." Abbott's work as a whole is a perfect example that tells us the lines are not so strictly drawn. Her documentary work in the Depression puts her firmly in the social realist school, yet her nighttime views of New York stand up quite well as purely formal photography.

Edward Weston shared Adams' lofty view of the proper role of photography, writing to him that, "It

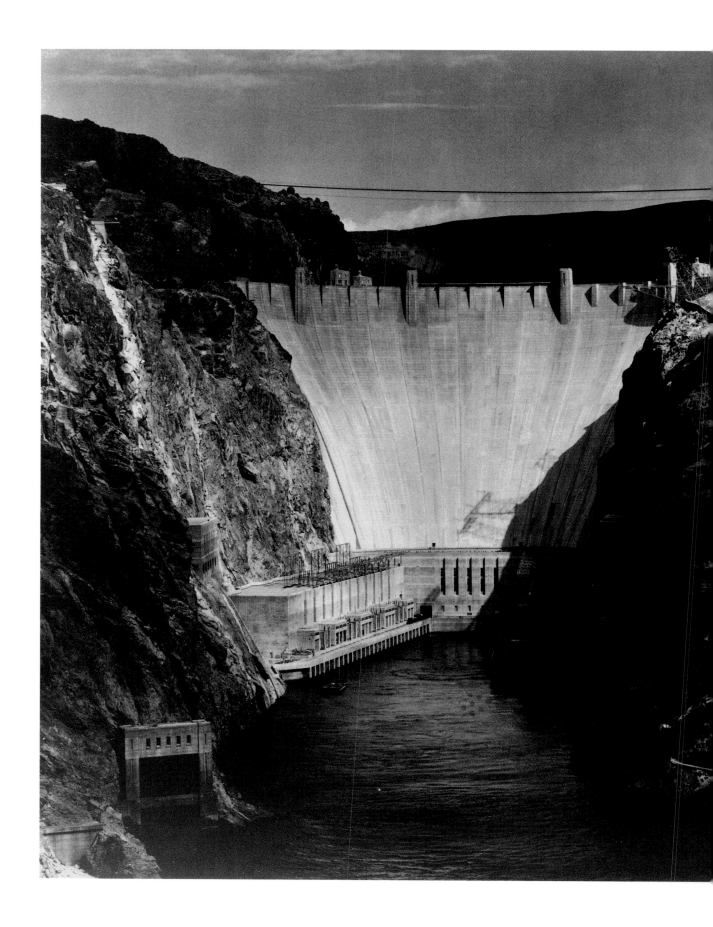

seems so utterly naive that landscape—not that of the pictorial school—is not considered of 'social significance' when it has far more important bearing on the human race of a given locale than the excrescences called cities." Weston, too, thought that the subject matter was not what determined the emotional reaction to a picture, but took the idea a little too far for Ansel with, for example, his picture of peppers that resemble entwined nudes. Ansel always felt that the subject should be dealt with matter-of-factly, that a rock should look like a rock and a vegetable, well, like a vegetable, not a nude. Ultimately, it remains a matter of seeing the world in differing ways.

Steichen and Stieglitz

Edward Steichen wrested control of the Museum of Modern Art's photography department away from Beaumont Newhall and installed his own vision of the future of photography. In his resignation letter in March 1946, a saddened Newhall wrote, "The Museum cannot have me if they have Steichen." Ansel felt that with Steichen's rise the museum had been turned over to vulgarians, and that it would soon become little more than a giant archive for subject photography.

Steichen's most visible move was putting on the famous "Family of Man" exhibit in 1955, perhaps the best-known photographic exhibit of its time. The volume *The Family of Man* is to this day a wonderful introduction to the expressive power of the subject in photography, but Adams detested the show for just that reason. Steichen wrote grandly in the introduction to the book that the show was "the most

Boulder Dam

The great concrete mass of Boulder Dam seems to fit neatly into the natural setting. The balanced composition, with the dam in the center and the highlight of the structure on the lower right, makes the dam look like an organic structure on the river. Power lines span the man-made horizon of the dam in this photo taken in 1941.

ambitious and challenging project photography has ever attempted," but Ansel felt that the expressive photography in the show suffered from a mediocre selection of images and the poor quality of some prints and enlargements, especially what he felt was a grotesque blow-up of his own print, *Mount Williamson*, displayed saccharinely with a picture of a child reaching out to it.

In July 1946, Ansel got a telegram from Nancy Newhall reporting that Alfred Stieglitz had died at the age of eighty-two from a stroke following a heart attack. A cremation ceremony at his beloved home in Lake George, New York, where he had taken so many masterful images, was attended by Georgia O'Keeffe, who was holding up well, Paul Strand, the Newhalls,

and Stieglitz's biographer Dorothy Norman, who was emotionally devastated.

For his part, Ansel was resigned to his mentor's death. He knew Stieglitz was unhappy at the end of his life and that this was better for him, but he was sad about the loss personally and for the world. At the time Stieglitz's reputation was in penumbra if not eclipse. Adams was concerned that his importance in the history of photography was being overlooked. "In a very definite sense, Stieglitz is photography," he once wrote Nancy Newhall. Stieglitz's stature as an artist, a champion of modernism, and a pioneer of low-light photography has been resurrected by more recent critics. History is continuously redacted by the living, for their own purposes.

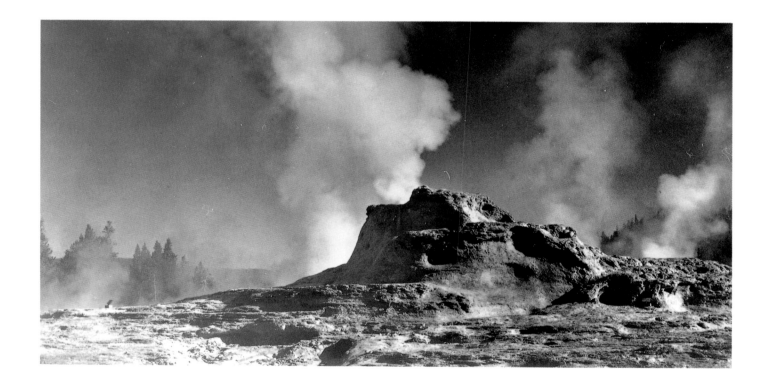

Castle Geyser Cove, Yellowstone National Park
A powerful, vertical column of steam sets off the sharply etched edges of the rock formation in the center of the image. Deep shadows define the rock face on the left, leading to highlights and the texture of broken rock to the right. Misty trees in the lower left of the frame and the broad expanse of sky add to the drama of the image.

Central Geyser Basin, Yellowstone National Park
Superb highlights make this hot spring's outflow appear like a river of molten silver. The range of tones is stunning, from the richly textured bank in the foreground to the pure white clouds of steam against the almost black ridge in the background.

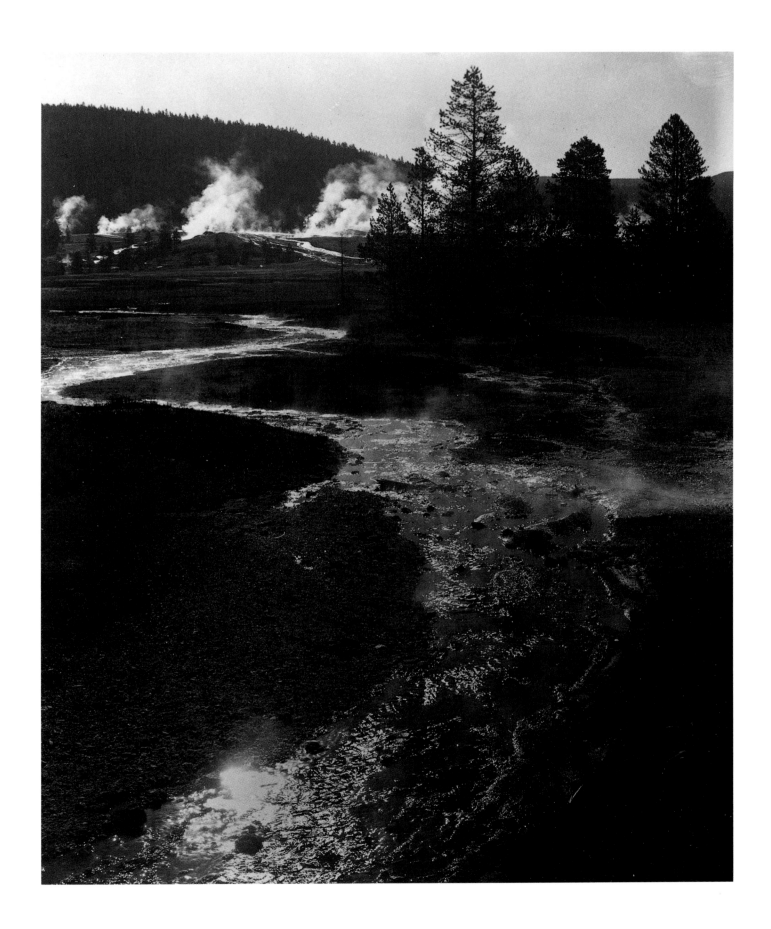

The Later Years

Ansel took far fewer photographs in the decades after the 1940s, concentrating his energies instead on teaching classes, organizing the major collection of his negatives in the Ansel Adams Archive at the Center for Creative Photography at the University of Arizona, and tirelessly promoting the cause of conservation in America. He never lost his fascination with new technological developments in photographic equipment, and was an enthusiastic supporter of the revolutionary inventions in instant photography by Edwin Land. Ansel believed that the Polaroid camera was an invaluable tool as a guide in sensitometry and in producing fine prints.

Adams remained an iconoclast to the end. He brought the attention of the White House upon himself in an interview with *Playboy* magazine (May 1983) in which he declared, "I hate Reagan." As a result the President invited him for a discussion of conservation issues. Ansel left the fifty-minute session unmollified, telling the *Washington Post*, "I got a feeling he doesn't have any fundamental interest or knowledge in the environment as a concept." Adams' final published letter, printed in *The New York Times* on March 4, 1984, was a plea to end the threat of nuclear war. Ansel died from heart disease the following month on April 22, at the age of eighty-two, near his home in Carmel, California.

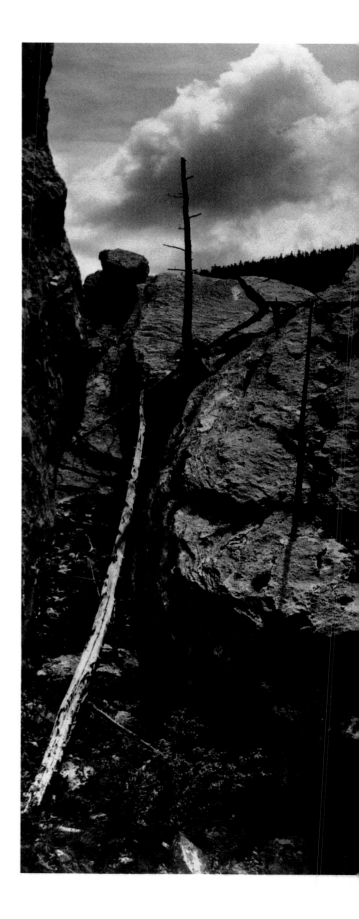

Rocks at Silver Gate, Yellowstone National Park
A single, rugged rock face dominates this plate, set against a dark slope and brilliantly highlighted clouds. The rock emerges out of a deep gray border at the bottom and the eye follows the pattern of dark crevices and shadows through the textured surface.

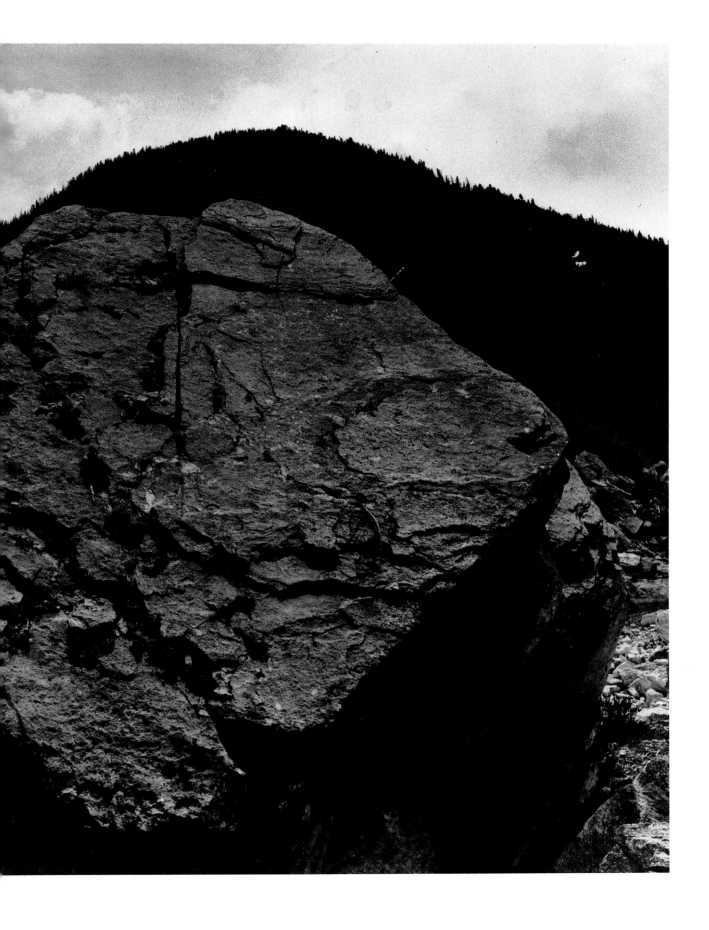

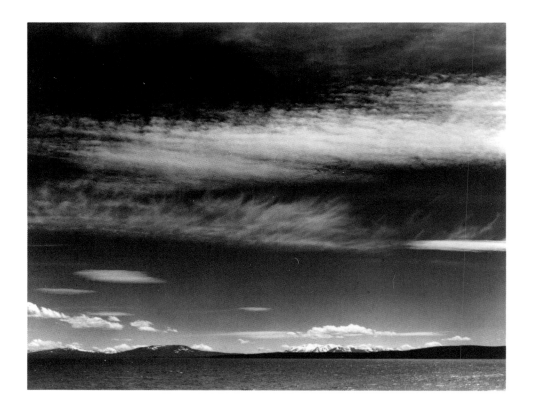

Yellowstone Lake, Yellowstone National Park

This plate expresses the sense of vastness and freedom of the parks' lands by framing windswept clouds high above minute peaks in the background. The image serves more as a purely emotional expression of the photographer's feeling about the landscape rather than a strictly documentary record of the parks. Ansel combined both aspects of photography in his mural series for the Department of the Interior.

Old Faithful, Yellowstone National Park

Adams' images of the west are markedly different from his nineteenth-century predecessors, such as Timothy H. O'Sullivan, in part because of a different sensibility but also because of different technologies. The film stock Ansel used was able to pick up details of blue sky more efficiently so that his skies are remarkably textured, whereas in the earlier images the skies are simply a burnt white. O'Sullivan's shadows are more luminous than Ansel's, but Adams was able to make use of the more intense contrasting quality of his film stock.

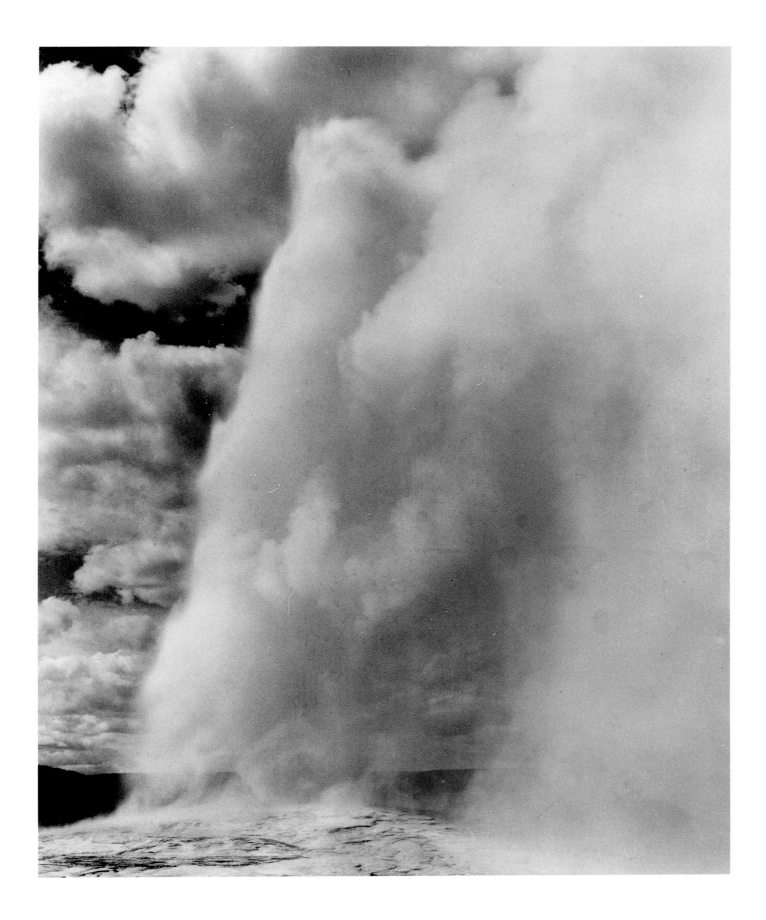

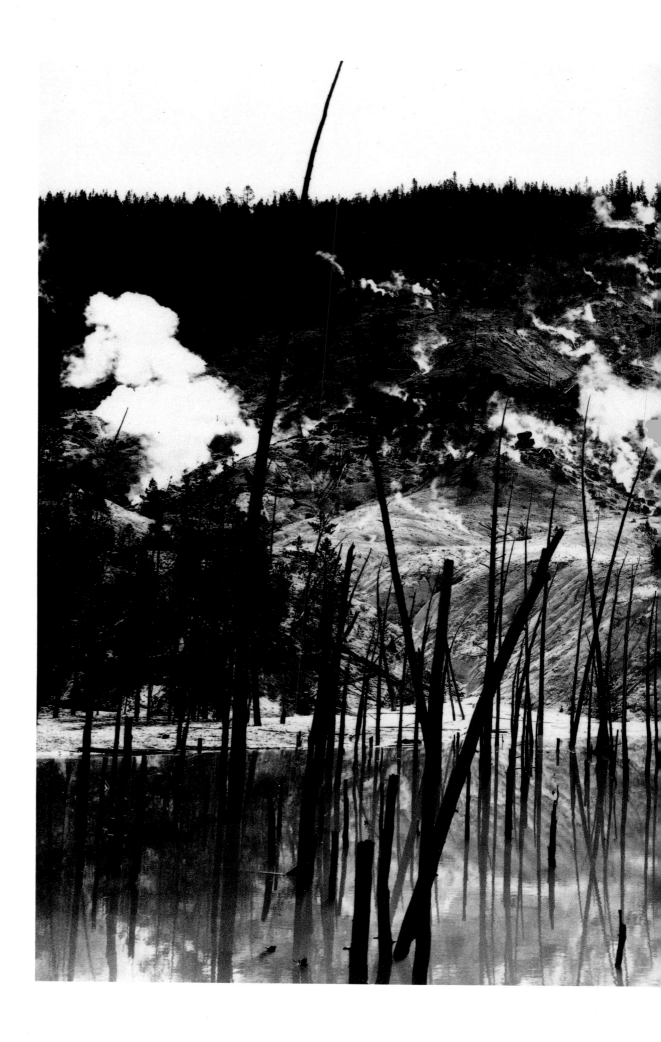

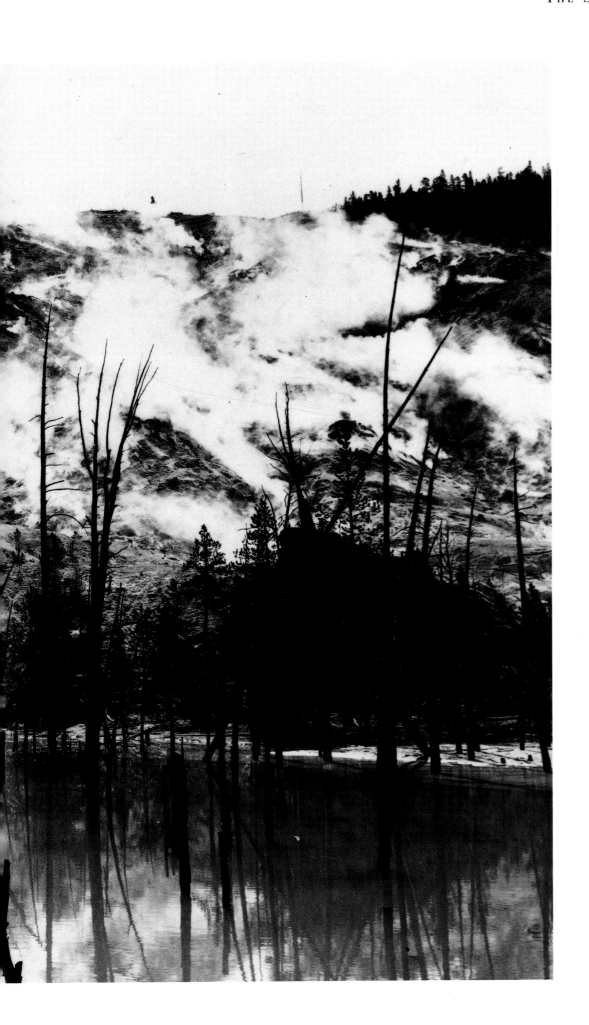

**Roaring Mountain,
Yellowstone National Park**

Ansel recorded the stark-
ness of the national park
landscapes, not just views
that would attract tourists.
He believed that the parks
would find their appropriate
audience without the need
for promoting activities
that did not relate directly
to the natural environment.

121

Old Faithful Geyser, Yellowstone National Park
In answer to critics who believed that photographs
were only interesting because of the subjects depicted,
Alfred Stieglitz, Adams' great mentor, took a series of
plates of clouds and sky and called them emotional
"equivalents" of what he was feeling. Later, he came
to believe this about all photography. Ansel's astonish-
ingly varied images of Old Faithful at different times
of day can be considered his own series of equivalents.

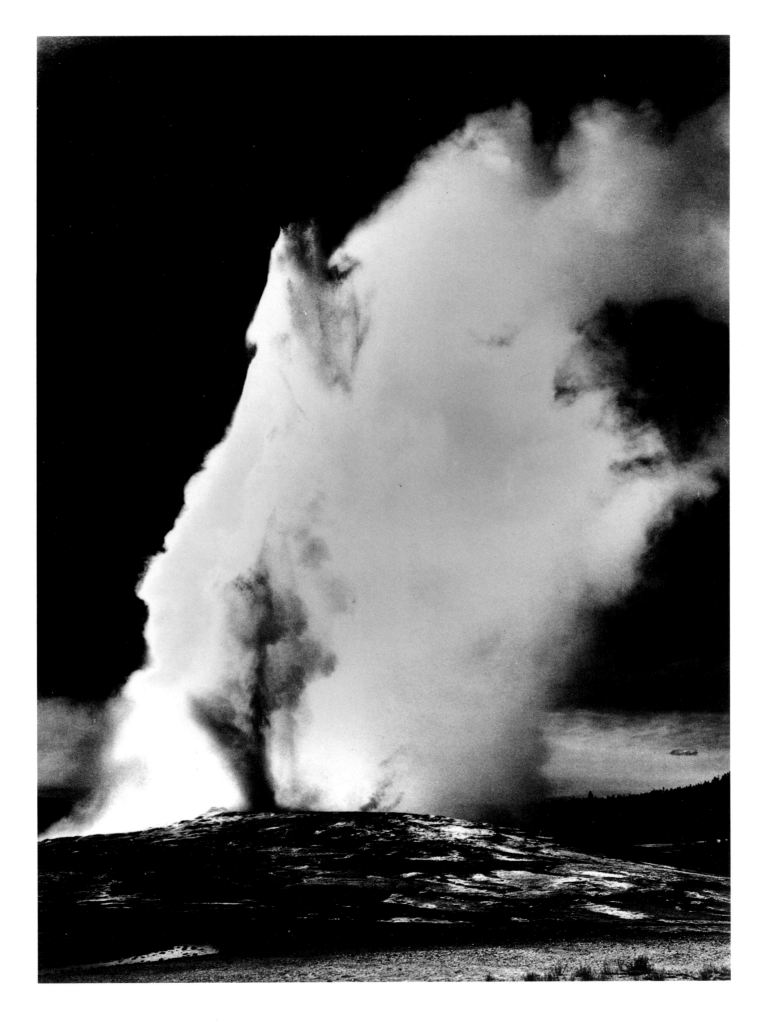

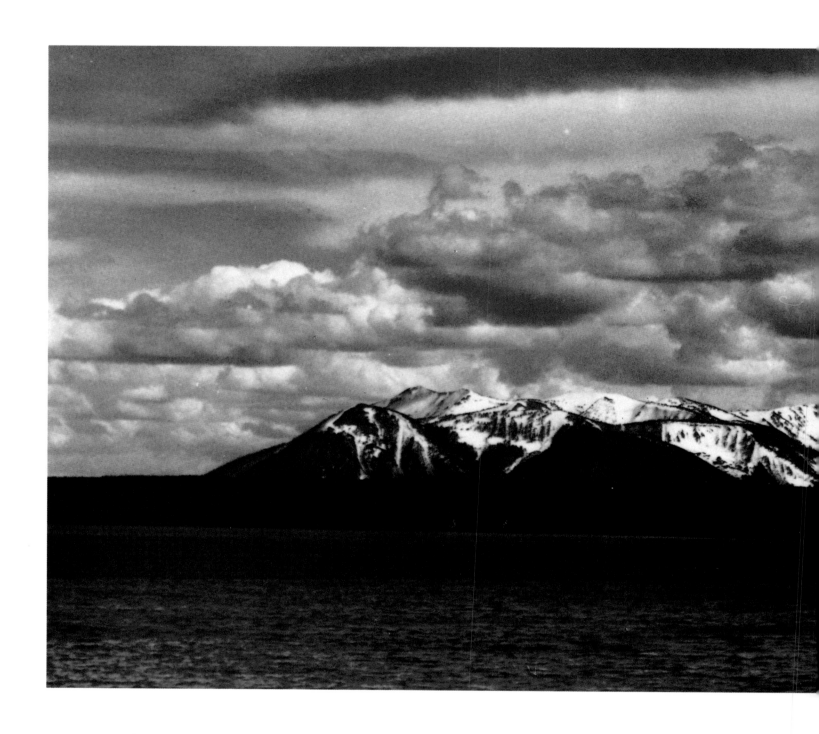

Yellowstone Lake, Mount Sheridan

Snow-capped peaks in the distance seem to echo the scudding cloud patterns in
the center of this image. The gray border of the lake at the bottom of the frame and
the long swaths of gray in the sky create for the viewer a symmetrical composition.

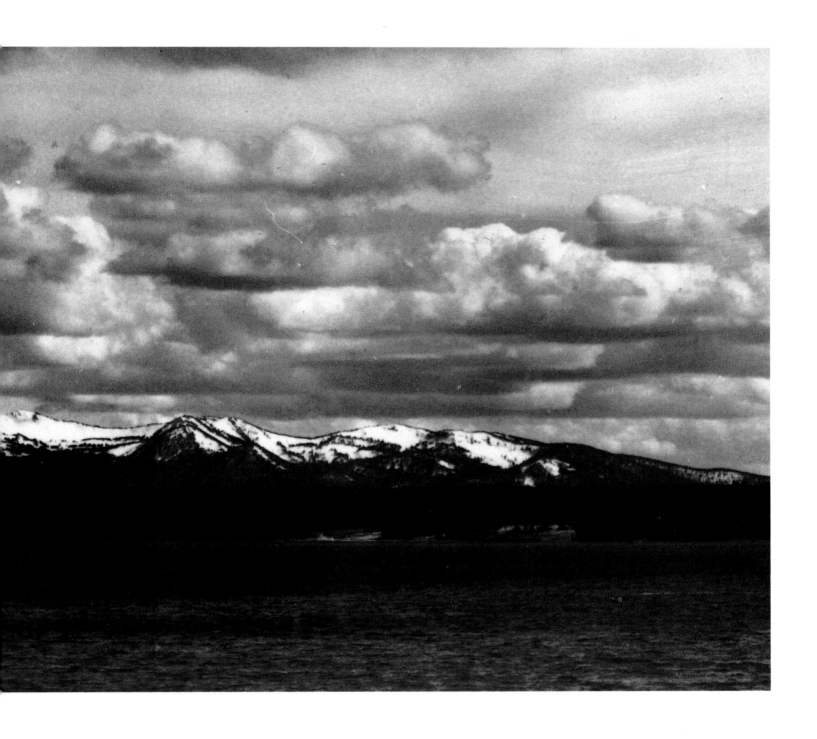

Yellowstone Falls
The force of the flowing cataract is expressed with a
long exposure that captures the motion of water. A long
lens flattens the composition into a steeply vertical series
of planes. Bold contrasts of the highlights of water against
the deep black rocks accentuate the power of the falls,
even though it is not the largest element in the frame.

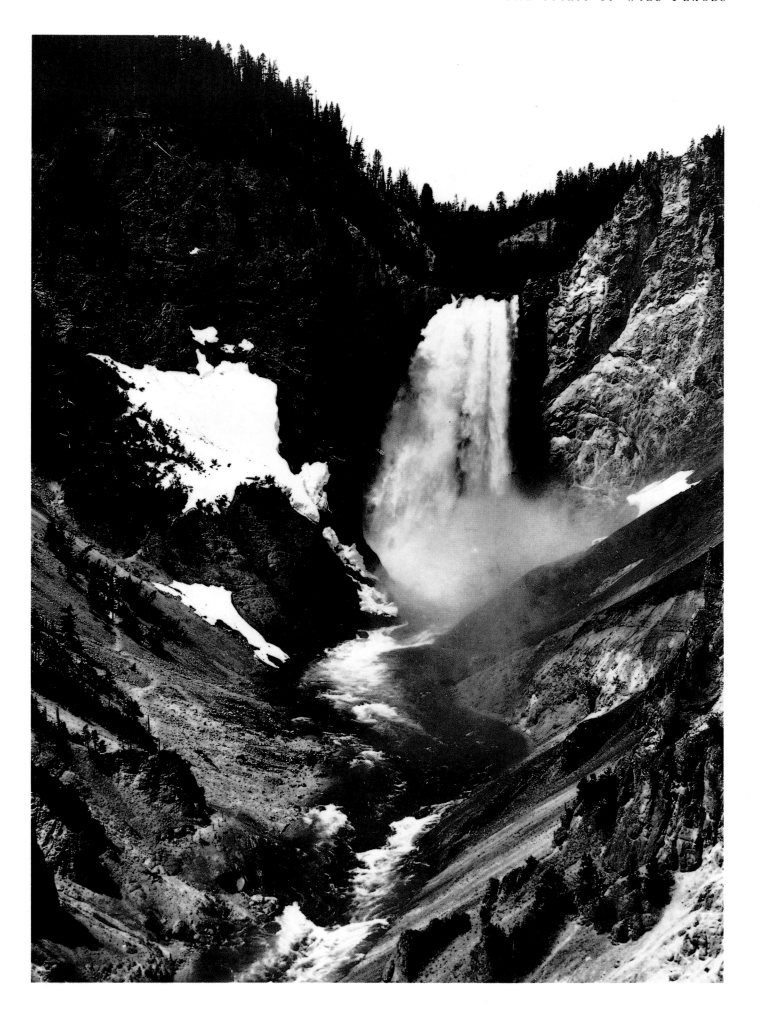

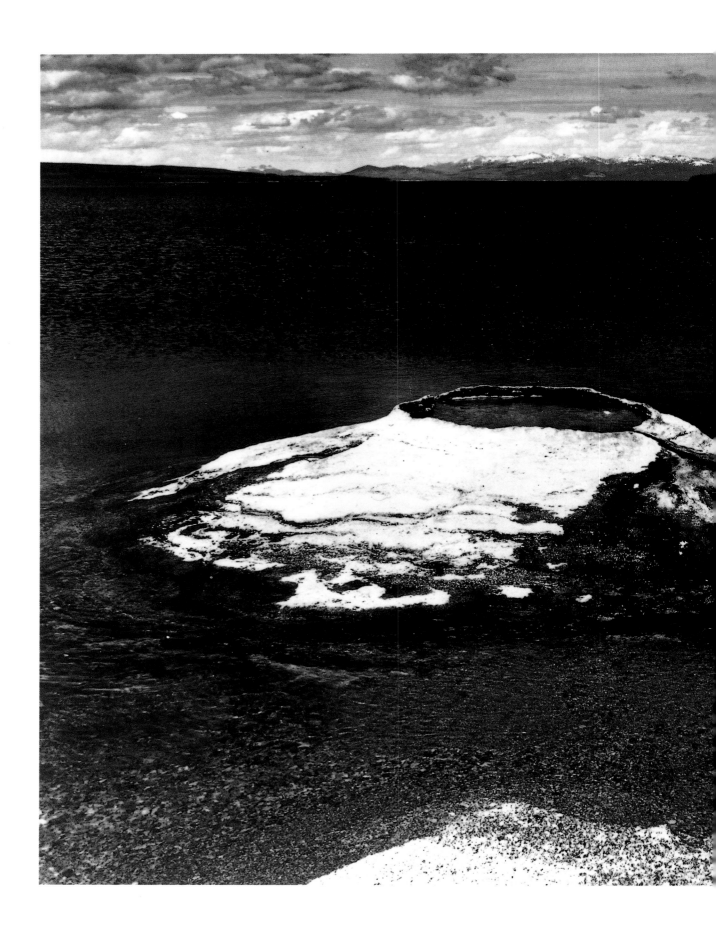

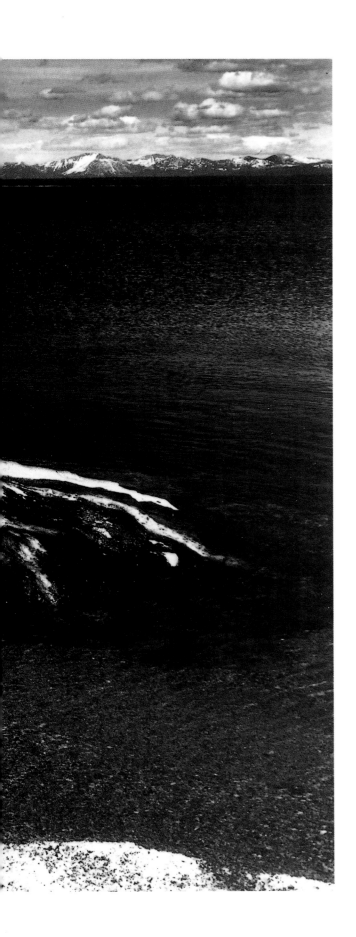

**The Fishing Cone—Yellowstone Lake,
Yellowstone National Park**

This image plays with a reversal of scale.
The unusual cone formation in the center
of the frame seems to dwarf the tiny range
of mountains on the horizon. The eye imputes
the scale of the far mountains to the central
formation and at the same time transfers the
sense of detail and texture from the foreground
to the background, melding into a detailed sky.

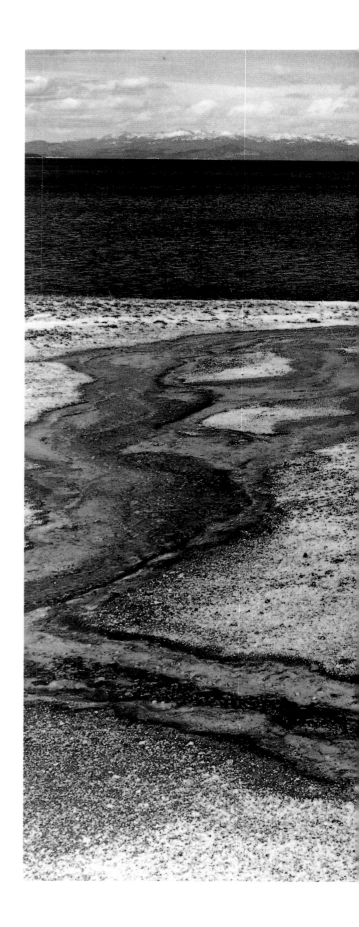

**Yellowstone Lake—Hot Springs Overflow,
Yellowstone National Park**

This wonderfully abstract image is an example of
Ansel's modernist sensibilities at work in the context
of photographing natural scenes. The scale of the
image is unexpectedly reversed; thus the hot spring's
overflow dominates two-thirds of the image, while
mountains form a tiny border. The texture and the
tonal range of the flow is almost machinelike in its strong
edges and fine detail, like a close-up of a sheet of metal.

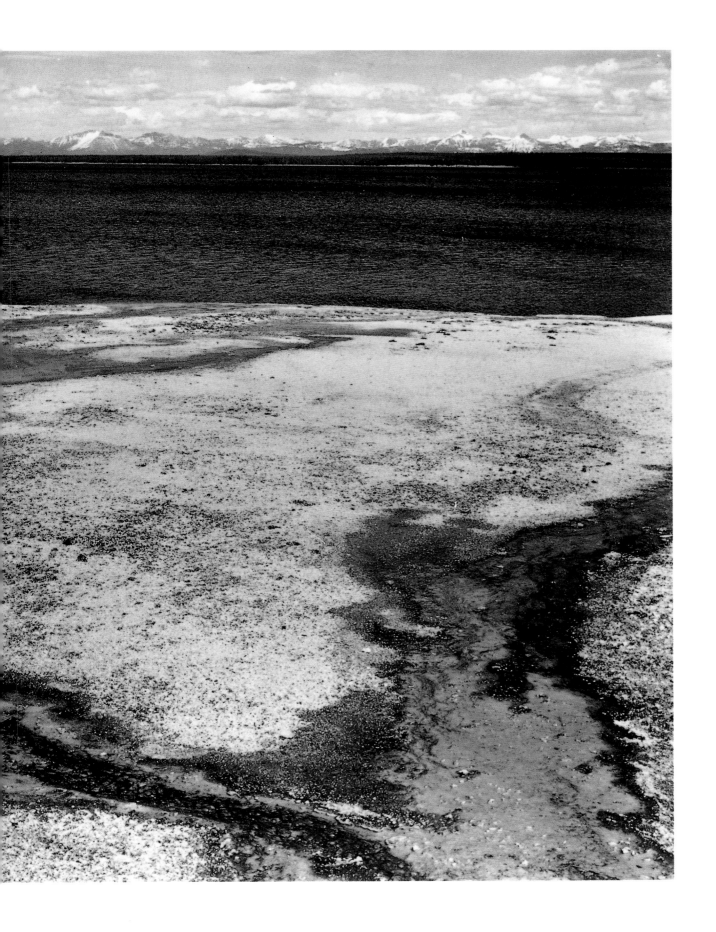

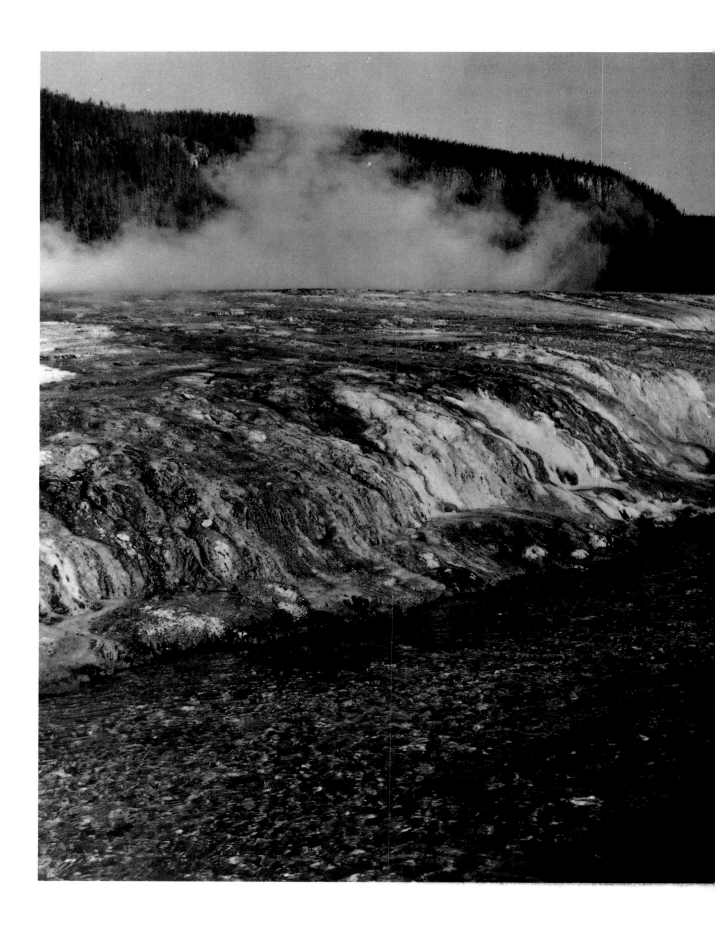

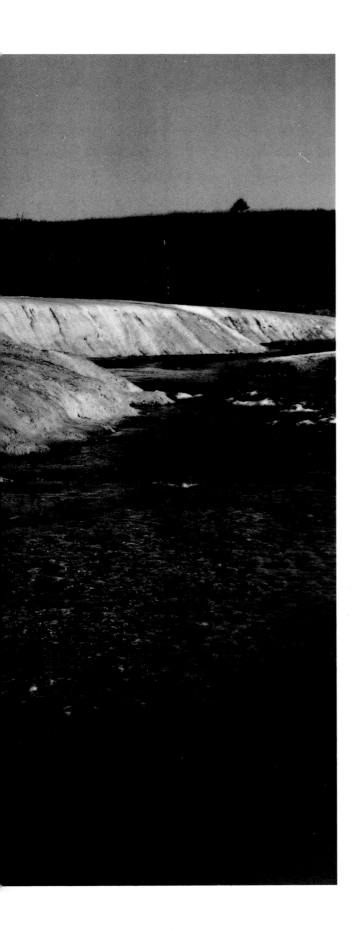

Firehold River, Yellowstone National Park
There is a tension in this image between its straightforward depiction of a river bank and its composition as strongly defined zones of tonal difference, from the clear sky to the line of dark trees obscured by the cloud of steam and the detailed textures of the bank and riverbed. The eye follows the diagonals to the distant details of the background to the right.

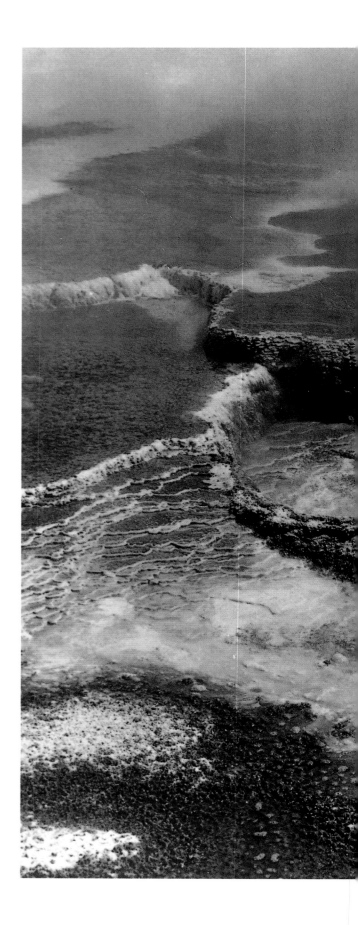

**Jupiter Terrace, Fountain Geyser Pool,
Yellowstone National Park**

This up-close view of a geyser pool emphasizes
its steamy, volcanic nature. There is an interesting
shift in scale here so that one is no longer sure
exactly how high these stone terraces are. It could
almost be a long shot of some primordial landscape
stretching into vast distances, like a Niagara Falls.
The complex rhythm of highlights makes the eye rest-
lessly scan the image for more clues to size and scale.

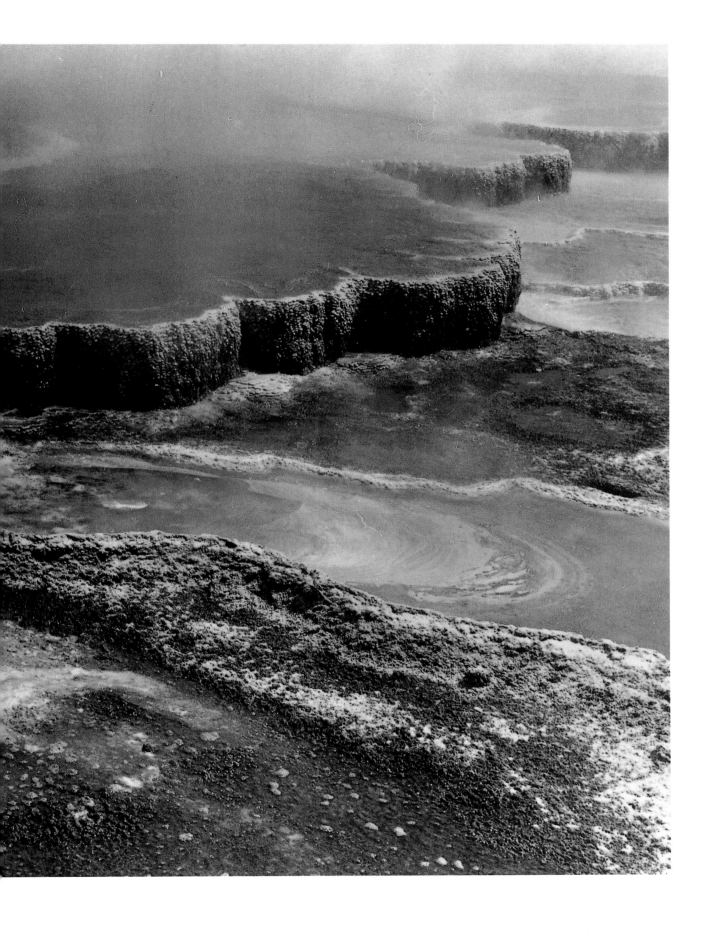

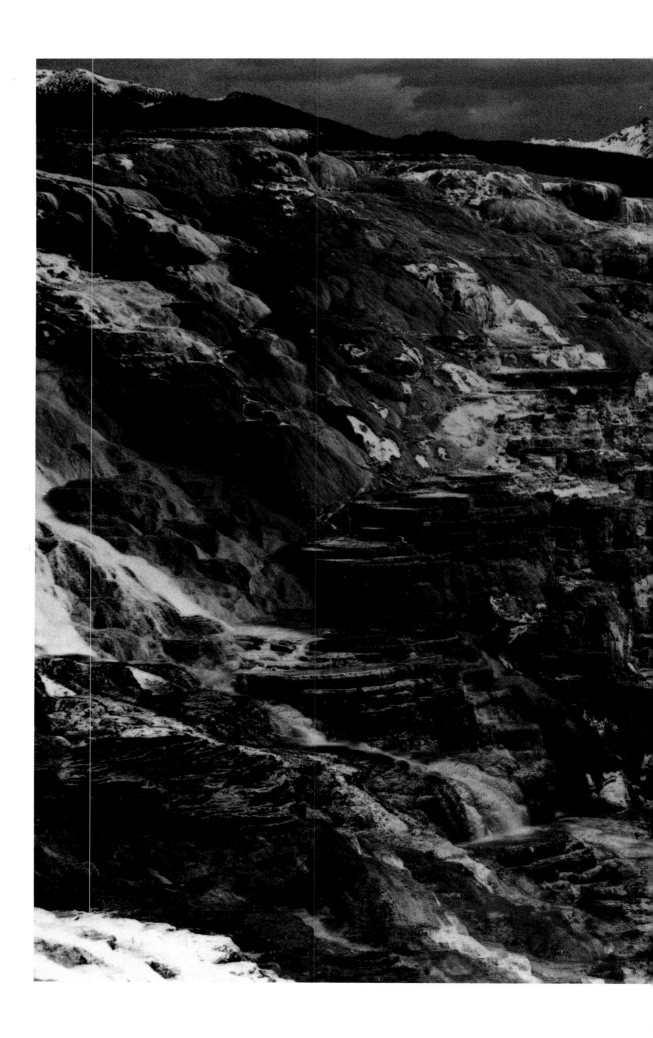

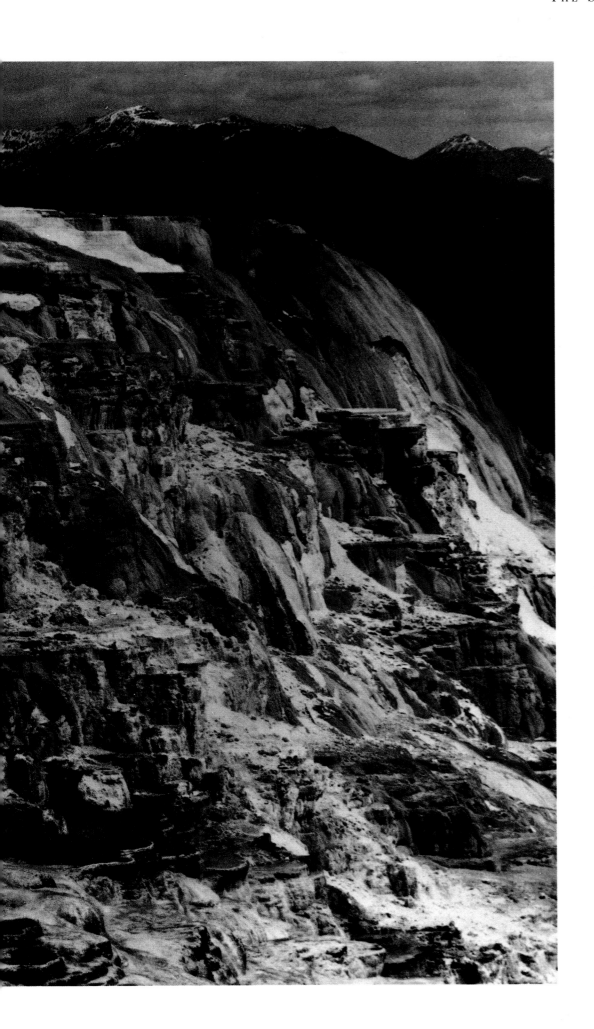

**Jupiter Terrace,
Fountain Geyser Pool,
Yellowstone National Park**
This is a wonderful, almost
Edenic view of the grandeur
of the earth without the presence of humans. The eye follows the softly flowing water
over the intricate interstices
of the pool. The downward
motion of the water is accentuated by the asymmetrical
frame, with the void of black
to the right. An overall effect
of the orderly, fugal quality of
natural images is completed
by the finely detailed snow
peaks in the far background.

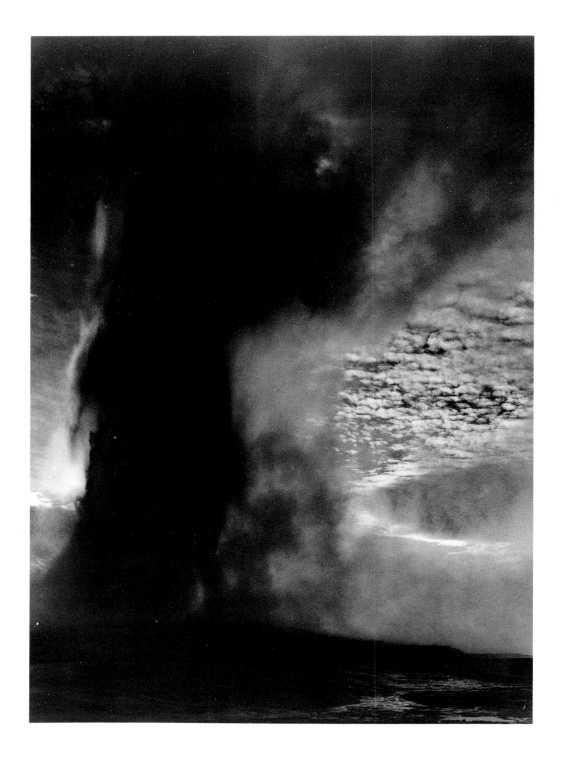

Old Faithful Geyser, Yellowstone National Park

The focus of the plate is not so much on the geyser itself, which appears as a somewhat indistinct gray mass because of the motion of water, but on the fine detail and highlights of the cloud cover in the background, which glistens like the scales of a fish. There is a tension between the orderly, detailed sky and the pulsing formlessness of the geyser.

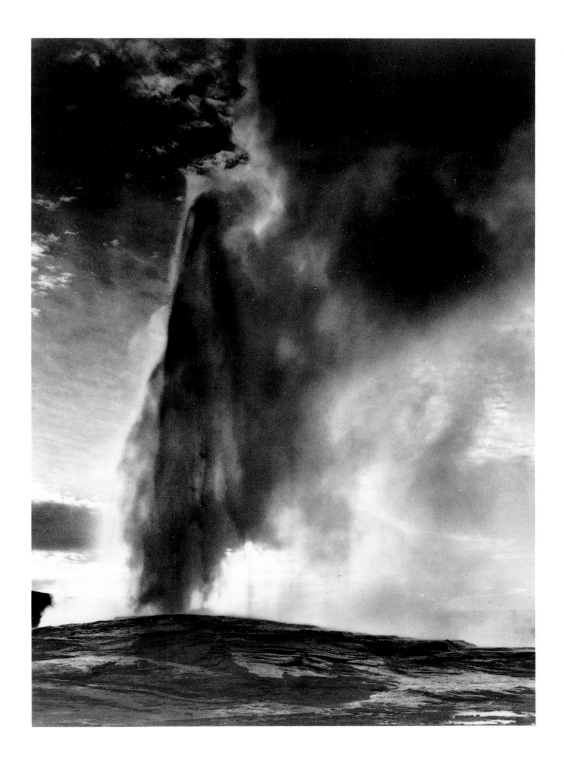

Old Faithful Geyser, Yellowstone National Park

This plate might have been taken moments from that of the
following photograph but it has a much different emotional
feel. The geyser looks less destructive because the dark
tones are not as opaque, and the sky looks less menacing
because of the reduction in extremes of contrast.

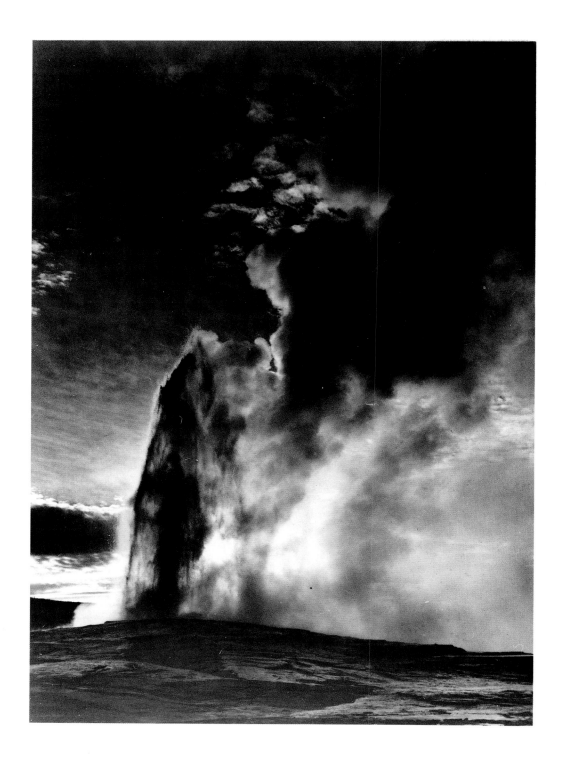

Old Faithful Geyser, Yellowstone National Park

The emotional impact of lighting and exposure are demonstrated in
the startling reversal of expectations in this plate. The geyser, which is
normally photographed in light tones in black and white, here appears
as a turbulent, inky fountain, reflecting the power of the darkened sky.

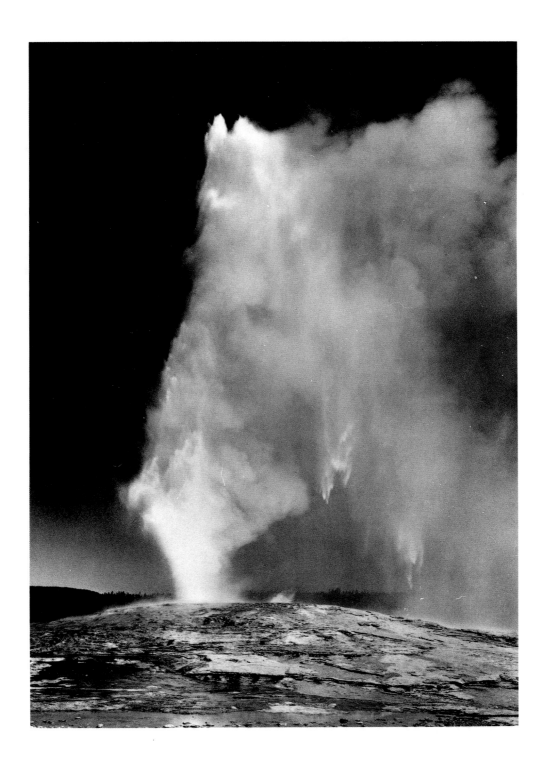

Old Faithful Geyser, Yellowstone National Park

This rendition of a dramatically darkened sky
is distinct among Adams' many images of Old
Faithful. The dark background brings out the
more abstract qualities of the play of water.

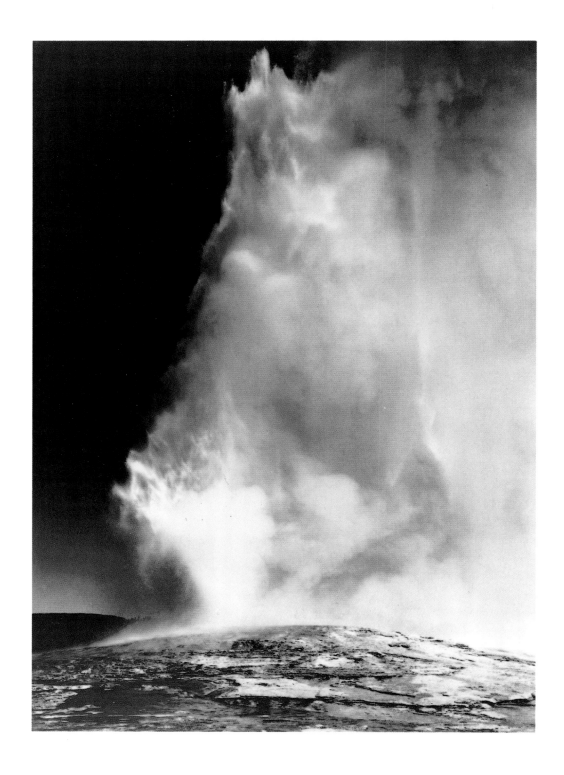

Old Faithful Geyser, Yellowstone National Park
The purer white tone of the geyser in this image emphasizes the powerful
vertical edge of water against the dark sky. The force of the geyser is
expressed by the hot spot of highlights in the center. The sensation of
water falling off in the wind to the right is conveyed by softer gray tones.

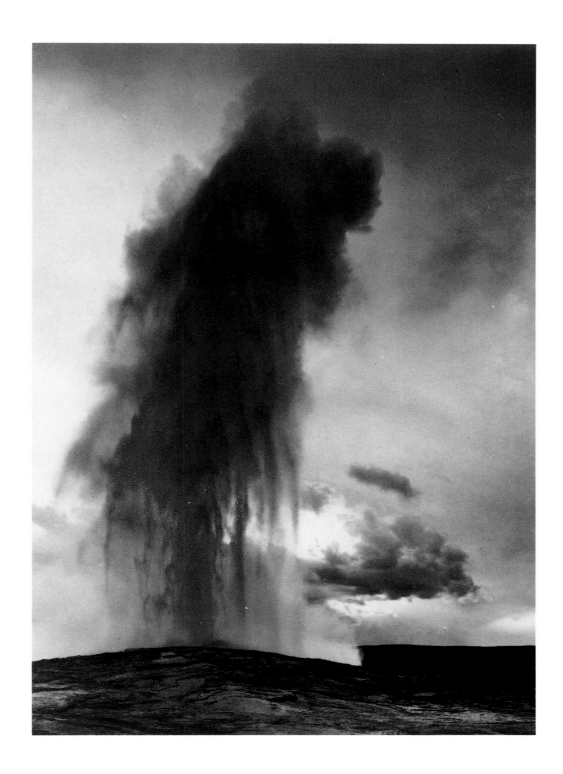

Old Faithful Geyser, Yellowstone National Park

The deep gray column of the geyser rises up from the dark foreground, which is in strong contrast to the silvery highlights of the earth in previous plates of this image. A low-lying cloud with highlights in the center emphasizes the verticality of the water column.

INDEX